FEISTY

DANGEROUSLY AMAZING WOMEN USING THEIR VOICES & MAKING AN IMPACT

RED THREAD PUBLISHING

For any woman who's ever been called:
Feisty
Uppity
Difficult
Dangerous
Unruly
Unreasonable
Bossy
Bitchy
Loud-mouthed
Wild
Too much
Too bold
Too anything
Or some other slur intended to make you feel ashamed of your untamed
perfection

You are a wonder, just as you are
and you are very welcome here.

CONTENTS

INTRODUCTION

I used to say *the world needs more feisty women.* But during this collaboration with the authors who share here, I have changed my mind.

The women of the world are plenty feisty. We are brave, courageous, resilient, and powerful. What the world does need is for women, the world over, to *know how incredible they are!* The authors of this collection are taking one powerful step to open the conversation, to give permission to others to rediscover their natural feistiness.

The goal of this collection is to give inspiration to others to reignite their childlike authenticity, to embrace their natural, healthy, independent uniqueness, their boldness, their silliness, their innate ability to know and speak for what's right, to act in alignment with their true selves.

At this moment, my six-year-old daughter is playfully splashing in the pool, fully embodied. She enjoys being a human in this world. She feels safe and comfortable in her body. She enjoys dressing up, dancing wildly in front of the mirror, singing at the top of her lungs. She is opinionated and vocal; she knows herself. She is confident, knows what she likes and what she doesn't like, and holds nothing back. She expresses when she is sad, angry, hurt, or frustrated. She's also quick to be joyous and silly.

Each of us came into this world with all the natural abilities to be sassy, feisty, fearless, and proudly ourselves. Sadly for many of us, we lose it. It is beaten out of us literally or metaphorically and a vibrant wild part of us withers.

Take this book and the journeys shared here as an homage and permission for you to re-embrace this part of yourself that may lie dormant, having become stagnant, shamed or scared out of you.

Each author takes a risk by sharing her story—some brave, some inspirational, some terrifying—stepping into her voice and into her experience. She takes this risk with each of us in mind. We are stronger together. None of us is in this alone.

When we share our stories and let others in, we create an unbreakable bond. Individually, we grow into our truth; collectively we stand side by side, highlighted by our common experience and our mutual respect, our appreciation for one another in both what unites us, and what keeps us unique.

It is my truest hope that by reading our stories, you find a little bit of yourself in these pages, also that you experience something well outside your own understanding; find empathy and compassion for others and for yourself.

More than that, it is my trust that you will discover and reignite your own confident feisty and cultivate the superpowers within yourself that both you and the world need, now more than ever.

YOU HAVE NO POWER OVER ME

MAKING THE MOST OF OUR FEISTY FLICKERS

BY ADRIENNE MACIAIN, PHD

E very woman I know has at least one Very Scary Dragon story.

You know the one: where your agency is stolen from you and guarded by a Very Scary Dragon.

In every such story, though, there are Feisty Flickers: moments of sudden clarity that, despite all evidence to the contrary, your agency is, in fact, still yours.

It's that fire that sparks behind the eyes of an elephant who tugs on its chain just hard enough to realize the tiny post that once kept it trapped is no match for it now.

It's that moment at the end of Labyrinth, when young Sarah looks into the eyes of Jareth, the Goblin King (a Very Scary/Sexy Dragon indeed), and remembers the final line of the play she'd been rehearsing, which also just happens to be the key to escaping his labyrinth (and no doubt every other illusory trap she will find herself in throughout life):

 "You have no power over me."

This moment is not the Big Boss Battle, when we must finally fight the Very Scary Dragon to regain our freedom. But that moment could not be possible without this one.

The Feisty Flicker is the moment we finally become willing to *resist*. When we screw up our courage and opt, instead of appeasing our Very Scary Dragon as usual, to give it the metaphorical finger, consequences be damned.

And consequences there will be. But in that brief flicker of feistiness, we remember that we are free to act, regardless. And act, we do. Even if that action is choosing NOT to act in the way we're expected to.

Like the time I chose *not* to use the ticket to Paris bought for me by the director of an indy film I was slated to star in. That probably sounds like a terrible decision until you find out that he'd snuck into the contract that we were to share a hotel room ("like husband and wife," he wrote in a subsequent email) throughout the course of the rehearsal and filming process.

Non, merci.

I've had many such Feisty Flickers in the course of my life. If you've read my books or listened to the That's Aloud podcast, you're already familiar with a few.

One of them, described in the "Authenticity" chapter of *Release Your Masterpiece*, involves a Very Scary Dragon just about all of us have to face up to at some point: Shame.

POUR SOME GLITTER ON IT

I'm fourteen years old. My very first boyfriend has just broken up with me via locker note after accidentally walking in on me (along with his best friend and mine) in the act of self-pleasuring with the aid of a DIY sex toy and a girl-on-girl Penthouse spread.

Whatever reputation I may have previously possessed has just died a sudden and spectacular death at the hands of the jr. high rumor mill, and my life has descended into an infernal abyss of nonstop bullying and harassment.

So here I am in the girl's bathroom, shaking uncontrollably, mentally eliminating escape routes and coming to terms with the fact that there is no avoiding the shitstorm ahead. The only way out is through.

"If you can't hide it," I tell my harried reflection in the warped metal mirror, *"pour some glitter on it."*

That's when I grab my notebook and, willing my cheap ballpoint pen to become mightier than the sword, compose the first of what is to be many lists of prepared comebacks.

At first, they come slowly, almost painfully, as if I am translating them from a language I barely know and haven't spoken in years. Perhaps the one my sister and I invented for secret communications in the wake of one of our parents' infamous knock-down, drag-out, china-smashing screaming matches. But after a while, the snark starts to pour out of me thick and fast, like a 4 PM Colorado rainstorm in June. A gushing fountain of sassy esprit de l'escalier in advance.

Soon enough, I lose myself in the creative flow of the task. Snappy one-liners morph and grow into veritable monologues:

"Wow! Now there's one I haven't heard before. So clever! So cruel! Did you come up with that yourself? I would offer to shake your hand but, well, you know where it's been. Ha! So good. I'm gonna have to write that one down before I forget it. *grabs notebook and pen, journalist-style* Now, is 'lesbo' spelled with an 's' or a 'z'?"

I wouldn't go so far as to say I am enjoying myself. But for the first time since "the incident," I feel a glimmer of that sparkle they've worked so hard to make me ashamed of. And in this moment, it is enough.

A MARBLE-OUS REALIZATION

I'm standing among the Greek and Roman statues at the Musée d'Orsay in Paris.

I secured this trip to Europe as part of a shrewd negotiation with my father in exchange for gaining back the frightening percentage of my body weight I lost to an eating disorder my senior year of high school. But just because I went to the group counseling sessions and submitted to the weekly weigh-ins and constant surveillance doesn't mean I'm actually in recovery. All it means is that I've been willing to play along thus far in order to get what I want.

And here it is. Here *I* am, in Paris, the city of love and light, taking in some of the most beautiful and celebrated artworks of European antiquity, when something altogether unexpected happens.

Walking through the rows and rows of statues of naked female forms--the ample hips and rounded bellies, the small, perky tits, the high foreheads and prominent noses--I feel an eerie sense of recognition. Aside from the fact that they've been carved out of marble and are thousands of years old, these pear-shaped ladies could pass for my sisters.

And these statues are not a catalogue of models the artists rejected as not-good-enough. They weren't told by an agent, "You've got an interesting look, but you're too short for runway and too angular for print. If you want to make money at this, lose ten pounds and get a nose job." On the contrary, these are portrayals of nymphs, goddesses, and the most beautiful human women the Earth had to offer at the time.

Standing here, amongst my stone sisters, I realize, for perhaps the first time in my life, that I am beautiful. Exactly as I am. No starvation or deprivation or beauty products or expensive trips to the salon or the fashion boutiques required.

I am naturally gorgeous, as it turns out. At least according to these long-since-dead artists. And why should I give their opinion any less weight (pun intended) than people who get paid to make me feel inadequate?

Suddenly, it isn't my father I want to rebel against. Or my doctor. Or any of the people who actually care about me. It's the itty-bitty-shitty-committee inside my own head that tells me I'm not thin enough, not pretty enough, not *whatever* enough.

And just like that, I realize I'm starving. Didn't I see a crepe stand on the way in?

THE STARING CONTEST

I'm strolling down the Pearl Street Mall in Boulder, Colorado with my friend Bret, when I see something, or rather someone, that yanks all the air from my lungs. I squeeze Bret's hand, and he follows my gaze to the crepe stand where a very French-looking man in his late-20s is flirting with a gaggle of teenage girls.

"Is that... *him?*" he asks, "Stephane?"

I nod, apparently unable to speak.

But as it turns out, I don't need to elaborate. Bret, being one of the only humans on the planet to whom I have confided my rape story in the year-and-a-half since it occurred, immediately understands my reaction and cheerfully offers to beat the living shit out of him for me.

Having recently passed his black belt test in some martial art or other, I know Bret is up to the task, and I take a moment to consider this generous offer.

"No thanks," I manage to say. Stephane's pain, I understand, would not negate my own. But when, a moment later, Bret makes a different offer, one intended to inflict psychological rather than physical damage, it's an offer I can't refuse.

In fact, I don't even want to. I wanna watch that oily piece of Euro-trash *squirm*.

You see, I've already gone to "the authorities." They asked me what kind of underpants I was wearing at the time (white cotton briefs), and, in the absence of any witnesses or physical evidence (all my traumatized 16-year-old self wanted to do in the wake of that nightmare was to scrub myself clean of it), advised me not to press charges. Short of allowing my friend to get himself arrested for assault on my behalf, my options here are limited.

So we make our way to the bench directly across from the crepe stand where my rapist is making small-talk with a veritable smorgasbord of potential victims. And we sit. And we stare.

It takes him a moment to realize he is being watched. Soon enough, though, he becomes distracted by our presence. He looks over at us. Once. Twice. Three times. He is trying not to stare, or at least, not to be caught staring. An impossible task, given that we are brazenly and unblinkingly staring back at him.

A manic self-consciousness grips him as he realizes he is the starring actor in a drama the details of which remain obscure, and his mannerisms become exaggerated, frenetic. He laughs a little too loudly, gestures a little too wildly, and the bemused high-schoolers soon make their excuses and depart.

It is only when he is alone that he dares to stare back, and finally has the opportunity to piece together who I am, and therefore what I'm doing here planted on this bench, glaring at him with my black-belted friend by my side.

And that's when the real show begins.

He ducks. He actually ducks down behind the counter, as if that will stop me from recognizing him.

Seeing the futility of it, he then attempts to sneak out the back. Once outside the crepe stand, however, he is entirely exposed, and is reduced to pretending he needed a good stretch before skulking back inside to formulate a new plan.

Finally, he begins the process of closing up the stand, despite the fact that it's not even close to closing time.

In his agitated state, his intended departure devolves into a veritable comedy of errors. He knocks a bag of flour off a shelf. Metal bowls clang. As he attempts to clean up the mess he's now made, he slips, falls, and swears loudly in French.

In another state of mind, I would have laughed my ass off. But I am too filled with grim satisfaction to be amused.

He knows what he did. And he knows that I know what he did. I have made him genuinely afraid of the consequences of his own actions, and it is fucking glorious.

BY RUNNING

It's just after dawn, and I'm running at the *par cours* in Onex, a suburb of Geneva, Switzerland. For those unfamiliar, a *par cours* (literally "by running") is a series of exercise stations set up around a public park. I come to this one regularly, and diligently do the exercises at each station, before rewarding myself with a leisurely jog down to *La Jonction* - the place where the Avre and Rhone rivers combine in a dramatic green and gray swirl.

But this morning, something feels off. A heavy mist is clinging to the trees, and I have the unsettling feeling that I'm being watched. The hairs on my arms keep standing on-end, and every bird rustling in the undergrowth gives me a start. It isn't until I get to the third or fourth station, however, that I actually see a male figure materialize between two trees.

He has dark, curly hair, pasty-white skin, and he's wearing a navy blue and white striped shirt and a pair of dark jeans. His expression is blank and unreadable. The overall effect is that of a spectral mime.

Rather than stay and contemplate the mystery of his ghostly appearance, however, I take off for the next station to see if he will follow me.

At first, I don't see him. Relieved, I pick up the small wooden log designed to be held across the shoulders while doing squats, and get into position. But before I can even complete a full squat, I feel the jarring warmth of an unfamiliar hand on my crotch.

Gasping, I turn my head to see him standing there behind me, his dark eyes empty and impassive. He seems to be waiting to see how I will respond.

Much to our mutual surprise, I respond by whirling around, log still in hand, and whacking him across the chest with it as hard as I can manage. He stumbles backward, and as he struggles to catch his breath, I am off and running, not toward *La Jonction*, but toward the police station.

Pas aujourd'hui, I pound out in my head, to the rhythm of my feet against the pavement, *not today*. Another day, I might have just run home and dissolved into sobs. But today, I'm feeling feisty.

Fuck you, Creepy Mime. You're goin' *down*.

ONE GOOD REASON

It's the middle of an ordinary night, and my husband has just woken me up for yet another round of "Give me three good reasons not to kill you right now."

This is one of his favorite games. He grabs a pillow, wields it menacingly, and demands I come up with three satisfactory justifications for my continued existence, *or else.*

This is surprisingly challenging, especially when yanked unceremoniously out of a deep sleep. Usually, though, I manage to come up with the requisite three reasons, and am then treated to an impassioned lecture on all my many failings as a wife, after which I can mercifully fall back asleep.

Tonight, though, I am straight up drawing a blank.

I mean, honestly, *is* there any good reason for him not to kill me right now? At least then it would be over, this extended psy-ops torture chamber masquerading as my marriage.

I've already tried, and failed, to leave him several times, and have grimly accepted by now that I am in it "til' death do us part."

And we both know whose death it will be.

So I go off-script. I say something that is definitely NOT on the list of approved reasons I should continue to exist. Something which, some part of me is all too aware, will piss him off royally.

"I pay our rent," I hear my voice saying. As if it is someone else's. As if this were some strange performance art piece being performed in my bedroom at 1 a.m., and not my life.

"Ah bon," I hear him growl, like an engine revving up. And that's exactly what he's doing. He's revving up his anger-engine, building up steam for the cinematic climax of batshittery he's about to unleash upon me.

But by the time I realize just how far over the edge my impulsive improvisation has driven him (or rather, has allowed him to rationalize driving himself) it is too late. The pillow is over my face, and every other thought is driven out but this one:

No, wait! I want to live!

At that moment, I realize that my blasé acceptance was a false front, designed to disguise the dangerous truth. There may not have been three, but there was definitely one good reason for him not to kill me that night:

I wasn't going to let him.

Those who have read *Melting Ivory* know what happened next.

But what happens after those moments of agency is not the point. I wasn't cured of my eating disorder that day at the Musée. That took decades of self-work and guided support. And though I eventually overcame every one of these Very Scary Dragons and went on to thrive, I'm sorry to report that, despite my best efforts, neither Stephane, nor the handsy *par cours* mime, nor my ex-husband were ever held fully accountable for their actions.

Regardless, the outcome doesn't negate our flashes of bravery. Quite the opposite. The fact that we are willing to stand up for ourselves in those moments, even in the subtlest of ways, despite the very real consequences to come, is what makes them magical. And the more we can recognize those moments from our own past, the more likely we will be to walk into future moments with full awareness and agency, and to make the most of that magic.

So I hope you'll take the time to illuminate a few Feisty Flickers from your own life, and share them with your chosen team, encouraging them to take back their own agency from whatever Very Scary Dragons are plaguing their life. You never know whose life your story may save, or what invaluable connections your vulnerability may forge.

Not sure who's on your team, or what stories to share with them, or how? Please reach out! I'm here to help you release the magic within.

More importantly, I hope the next time you are presented with an opportunity, however inconsequential in the grand scheme, to honor your intuition, stand your ground, and stick it to the Powers That Be, that you will grab that moment with both hands, look your dragon straight in the eye, and tell it the unvarnished truth:

"You have no power over me!"

About the Author

Adrienne MacIain, PhD, aka the Story Whisperer, is an author, educator, and inspirational speaker who helps struggling SOULopreneurs, freelancers, and unhappy employees transform into successful innovators by guiding them through her powerful Release Your Masterpiece process, and by matching up visionaries and creators via the Innovators' Guild (join here: https://discord.gg/uwSHCBHj9D) so they can collaboratively solve the world's problems with ease and enjoyment.

https://linktr.ee/adriennemaciain

TO THE OTHER SIDE

BY STACY DYSON

I can tell you exactly when I found my voice.

Well, the start of it, anyway. I was sitting in the San Diego airport, waiting for a flight to Las Vegas and chiding my Italian about-to-be-lover for 1. not handling his time well and 2. screwing up yet another chance to wish me away for a weekend of (as someone's grandmother...not mine...would say) "commencin' and carryin' on."

I told him we would get together when I got back. It was a turn-around trip; I would be home and ready to while away the better part of a week with him in 72 hours.

I was happy in the Before Times. Doing business, getting my love life back on track after far too long an absence, feeling balanced. Cloud 9 be damned; I was on Cloud 27, with clear sight and directions to Cloud No. 36.

I flew out of San Diego on a Tuesday, to a women's conference in Las Vegas. By the time I got back on Thursday, San Diego and most of the world had gone into total shut down. No assignations with my lover til Lord knew when, no gigs for the foreseeable future. Hell, I couldn't even go grocery shopping. I was well and truly trapped.

Not to worry, I said to myself. I can tough this out. A few months was all it would take to sort things, right? A few months… ANYBODY could handle that.

But time stretched and stretched and stretched... and not a damn thing changed.

No, that's not true. Everything / too much was changing. And with every shift of the time and tides, I felt more powerless.

The old folks say, "Let me tell you how it came to be." My Southern cousins say, "What had happened was..."

I'm just going to tell you to grab a beverage and hang on.

You might want to stretch for this.

Along with COVID numbers, racism bloomed. I'm of an age to remember the remnants of Jim Crow in public places. It was supposed to be different…

Then, Breonna Taylor died. I cried, could not stop crying, for two days. My heart would not, could not stop hurting.

Then, the video that flew 'round the world… a white cop kneeling on the neck of a Black man who was dying, pleading that he couldn't breathe. I couldn't, either. Day after night after every blessed week… I was exhausted. Frightened all the time, sick for this country and what it was doing to folks who looked like me. More names, more faces… every single day.

It wasn't just because I felt lost/betrayed/hopeless. My poetry, the voice I had always used to tough/bluff/survive the years wasn't enough to address this horror, these horrors.

"I woke up to find the world
my world
had stopped existing...
the way I've managed and lived
was disappeared...
Every day a new shattering of belief
every single day… ripped raw and quivering from
    my soul
Did you ever have something laying so hard on your
    heart

that you were fairly sure that to acknowledge it would
break you?"

— "CERTAIN MAGIC," *LOVELY AND SUFFERING*

I was living there, in that place where everything I saw and heard
lay like iron weight on my heart. And I didn't know what to do.

The streets one town over and my soul caught fire at the same
time.

I can tell you when that happened. It was another butterfly garden
day. Me sitting on the terrace, counting hummingbirds, trying to stay
cool with yet another iced drink, trying not to scream or cry or just
put my head down and give up. I'd been housebound for weeks,
trapped in what was, admittedly, a very pretty prison. The day itself
had been scripted by Satan; another story about another Black body
savaged by the police. It was the same story every day, from somewhere on the globe, but mostly here... arrests, beatings, murder done
for committing a BWB... being while Black. I was counting the
hummingbirds between teardrops, most days. Mired in depression,
trying to keep my head up while I was breaking down.

That particular day, that particular hour. Another shot fired,
another incident, another protest... and I couldn't take it anymore.
Would not take it anymore. No chance of getting out in the streets:
arthritis, COVID, and a household with a vulnerable population saw
to that. But I had to do something because everything I'd ever believed
was in disintegration mode; the world was breaking apart, and I had
to use my voice to make it stop. Make it change.

I wrote the poems on my phone. I'd never done that before, probably never will again. The screen was too small, and it was too hard to
make corrections. (There weren't many of those. I was writing
straight from my heart, and that sort of writing rarely requires an
edit.)

I started feeling a little less crazy. A little less powerless. I didn't
plan or search for the words; I couldn't have. I had never heard this
voice before. I let it take rein and run, while I held on for dear life. I

was doing what I was born to do. Write pure, write truth. Write regardless of what other people thought or would think… something I had flirted with before. Only a flirtation, because I used to think calm and steady diplomacy would get me where I wanted to go, show folks the light, preach the word without the possibility of alienating the congregation. All of that stopped mattering.

About now, some of you, (maybe all of you), are saying "Okay, so she changed her voice. What's so revolutionary and heart-stopping about that?"

Two reasons that this was a *major* risk.

First off, as a writer of any sort, but especially a poet who performs, you're apt to lose your audience if you suddenly change the way you say things or the style you write in. I was changing into a completely different mode and manner of expression. In the middle of a pandemic that was going to end Lord-knows-when. I had already lost a large share of my audience (and any potential audience), because I couldn't get out and gig. No gigs means no income. It equaled only teaching or editing, both of which are fine and noteworthy professions, but not anything I have a passion in. I was making a fundamental change in what my fans had come to expect, and the idea of losing my base was absolutely terrifying.

The second reason is that being a poet is not just what I do, it is who I am.

For me, words are more than pretty bits of imagining to manipulate; they are woven into my blood and bone. I don't just do this because I'm good at it—and I'm very, very good at it—I do it because I have to.

This was not a choice I made; nobody in their right mind wakes up and says, "Hey, I'm gonna be a poet!" To quote my business card, "I am a poet because there is no other way for me." Being able to sustain myself with writing and performance is icing.

I was getting ready to throw away the person/poet I'd been, change the mindset and manner that has fueled the way I navigate the world, the way I've sung and spoken since I was 5 years old. I was gambling with my *entire life*.

I sat on the terrace, every day, iced Coca-Cola on a country kitchen-themed napkin, laptop open and ready for one of the handful of virtual open mics I managed to book, or the blessing of a conversation with someone who was going as stir crazy as I was. I read the news and watched the videos. (As much as I could stomach. I never saw the Floyd video; I couldn't. I knew too many Black people who had lived that violence psychologically and physically, and I just couldn't. I listened to it, going into brief shock before I got sick to my stomach.)

> Let's talk about the night mares
> I mean, we've all had them
> dreams where all and everything is lost...
> I have never in my life waked up in tears
> gone to bed in tears
> knowing that there was no respite in sleep
> noting that whatever I woke to
> was going to be so much worse
> than what had numbed me enough to lose consciousness
>   the night before

— "THE WORST OF TIMES," *LOVELY AND SUFFERING*

I was writing because I was afraid that if I didn't, I would lose my mind. I was writing because it was the only thing keeping me breathing. This new voice was raw and uncompromising, had no worries of betrayal to audience or thoughts of diplomacy. It said what it needed to say, refused to apologize, and dared any backchat.

I kept getting messages from my friends and fans. They didn't recognize this voice, but they felt the urgency... and were a little afraid of the power. They were tagging me on Facebook and Instagram, urging other people to listen to what I was trying to say.

Which was that I was hurt. I was angry. I was feeling trapped and betrayed. All things I had never really admitted or alluded to... not in the voice I was using now.

My collection, *LOVELY AND SUFFERING*, was never meant to be anything more than another chapbook. I'd made the decision that it would be a year's worth of those patio poems, of that passion and pain and truth-telling, because I (naively, I grant you) thought the pandemic would be over with soon, and my work would serve as a remembrance to people about what we'd lived through. Besides, I reasoned, this poetic voice was surely an aberration. Fires like the ones burning now in my voice and my pen didn't burn very long. And (again, very naively), the things happening to women and Black people couldn't keep degrading. Things had to get better because things simply had to get better.

But the voice was there every day, forcing me to scribe in blood and fire. I remember leaning back in the garden chair, breathing deep as if I'd forgotten what free air tasted like. I was always shaking, always exhausted after I finished a piece.

It started to become blindingly clear that *LOVELY AND SUFFERING* was meant to be something bigger than a DIY chapbook that I ran up at the closest Office Depot. I won't bore you with all the details, only to say that I was lucky enough to find Sierra Melcher and Red Thread Publishing. That shaped the way things moved from then on. I was on a schedule, had the basic idea for the book firmly under control; while the incidents and feelings that created my subject matter weren't any easier to handle, at least the technical demands of making the collection into what my nephews called "a REAL book" made me feel less aimless, slightly less despairing.

I would very much at this point like to say I embraced the new choices, the new words, the new vision of what I could achieve. I would like to tell you that I rose up each morning, jubilant and singing, waiting eagerly for the cramping in my fingers to ease, so I could attack my keyboard and celebrate all that newness.

I would also like to tell you that I won $10 million from the Publishers Clearinghouse Sweepstakes and got a date with Antonio Banderas. But that didn't happen, either.

I was terrified. Nervous and nauseous. Sleeping really badly, because all I could think about was how I was going to survive an audience that saw / read the new stuff and said "What a load of crap. Why did she ever change what she was doing?"

I'd already gotten some mildly hostile pushback from folks who didn't know me, and fans who were... well, let's say confused, about the new path. In the meantime, the pandemic was grinding on and on and on, and I was getting really worried about the future of performance. I've been on stages since I was 19; I was looking at having to completely revamp a 40-year career that might include never being on a stage again. *Ever* again.

Right before I lost it for real, right before I got buried under the landslide of doubt and horror at what was happening in the world, right before I swore I could not take ONE MORE MINUTE, God decided to, as Ntozke Shange says, "Stop wipin' His feet in my face."

I can't tell you when, exactly. Only that I suddenly felt back in control of what I was doing. The new me was still getting settled, but I stopped fighting with her, let her be, let her figure things out. I could breathe a little easier. I started sleeping a bit better. The patio stopped feeling maximum lockdown, and became the launching- pad for ideas and meetings about new ways to get my work out into the world. The news reports and horrible stories were ever-present, but I could process them a bit—just a bit—more calmly now. The new voice started feeling like something I should have been breathing years ago.

A year later, and I'm still getting used to that voice... it takes twists and turns I'm not always ready for. I've learned to flow with it, not fight with it. My vision of how to be and who I am feels less foreign every time I do a virtual open mic, and the chat section blows up for 10 minutes. A lot of my old audience is hanging in for the ride/enthralled/enchanted/warming to the new style... and my new audience is growing exponentially/becoming international and cheering every move I make.

I am a poet...
it's a more difficult trick than one might imagine
    right now
I am trying to stick to necessary stories and
    illuminations...
The small excitements are beginning to wear my
    patience
I must be healing, then
because I want to rise from my dreams screaming in
    triumph
I want to run/singing.

— "AUGUST 14:44," *LOVELY AND SUFFERING*

That last line says all and everything. Tells the tale triumphant and true. Blesses the risk I've taken with my life and career. Marks me... *finally...* a free woman.

> *I want to run/singing.*
> *I want to run/singing.*
> *I want to run.*
> *Singing.*

About the Author

Stacy Dyson is a Black female poet who explores/ illustrates/ illu-minates the history, self-image, and philosophy of the Black woman.

Based in San Diego, she has performed/ workshopped in Okla-homa, South Dakota, New Mexico, Massachusetts, California, Nebraska, Texas and Colorado.

Author of six chapbooks and five spoken word CDs, her play FANNIE'S GIRLS: A 4-1-1 IN 5-PART ATTITUDE is a Colorado Women's Playwriting Festival winner. Former Poet Laureate for Imagination Celebration (Colorado Springs) and the CEO/lead poet of women's writing and performance groups DragonsWing(Colorado Springs) and Page to Stage: Women's Voices (San Diego), she was a 2009 Nominee for Poet Laureate for the State of Colorado.

Featured in venues all over San Diego, she's currently touring with her two new collections of poetry, *LOVELY AND SUFFERING* and *FOLLOW ME ON THIS*. Future projects include a new play titled *AUGUST 5000*, and an online women's writing/ performance group called FIRESCRIBE.

https://linktr.ee/stacydyson

MONDAY

BY MIMI RICH

MONDAY

I t's a Monday morning, early August 2014. It's been a week of hell, and it's not over yet.

I am back home in rural Calaveras County, California. Safe, but for how long?

For the first time in my long life, I have absolutely no idea what to do.

Should I try to go to work? My mirror tells me a resounding "NO." I still have two black eyes, open wounds on my temple and the back of my head and a swollen, broken hand.

What would my boss and colleagues think? How can I possibly function with such fuzzy thinking and tearful emotions? As Family Court Services Director at my local Court, how could I counsel divorcing clients in mediation when I am clearly a victim of domestic violence? Who am I to claim mastery over a subject that has clearly mastered me?

So I call in sick. And burst into tears—*again*—feeling as helpless as I have ever felt. My thinking is so confused. How can I proceed with my life? Somehow I have to face this one pivotal decision with only two outcomes:

    1. Try to forgive my husband Glenn for hurting me so badly, find a way to trust him again and recommit to our marriage

    -OR-

    2. Call the Sheriff, have my husband arrested and jailed as a felon.

The traumatized Me is so different from the usual confident, clear-thinking Me, the Victim a far cry from the rational Professional. Besides being a court mediator, I have been a psychotherapist for over thirty years. Until this situation (in my early 70's), my life has been blessedly trauma-free, my relationships kind, loving and respectful.

How did I get here? What am I supposed to learn from this fiasco? And what the hell do I do now? At this moment, I have in my hands the arc of the rest of my life and the fate of a man I (at one time) loved.

I feel completely alone. I feel shame for getting myself into this mess. Until I make a decision, there is no one I can talk to about my dilemma. I don't want to worry my family and close friends before I come to some resolution.

On this beautiful summer morning, while I am sobbing and so confused, the phone rings. It is my daughter Sierra calling from Colombia, South America, where she has lived and worked as a single woman for many years.

I pull myself together to be the supportive Mother. She and I have been talking about living together there in Medellin after my retirement and divorce, and I expect another brainstorming session.

But nothing could have prepared me for her surprising news: she is expecting a baby!

I feel unconditional elation. There is no discounting that a brilliant light enters my darkness at that moment and that a completely unexpected freedom beckons.

Suddenly my current situation is infused with joy and hope. Suddenly, everything is different. Priorities shift and clarify. My only child—and HER child—need me. A new vision, a new future opens before me, as it is opening for Sierra.

She has no idea what my past week has been like, and I am not ready to tell her. I don't want to worry her. But my confusion has lifted and my choice is now completely clear.

I think: *I NEED BACKUP.*

BACKUP

Feeling I still need some professional advice, I am lucky to find a therapist, Tamara (in the next county since I am friends with all the therapists in this county). She can see me today. She takes one look at me, hears a bit of my story, and says:

"You have to call the police."

In my traumatized state, I just needed another Wise Woman to push me toward what I know is the only choice. I drive directly from her office to the Sheriff's Department.

Two officers take my report, examine my wounds, urge me to spend the night in hiding, and accompany me to my house so I can pack some clothes.

Kind neighbors take me in for the night. Glenn keeps calling to check on me. It's scary, but I reassure myself that he doesn't know where I am. He only gets the home answering machine (our cell phones don't work in the country.)

That night, I telephone my boss to let him know that the "family emergency" that prevented me from working all last week was my own domestic violence situation. While he is not exactly a "warm and fuzzy" kind of guy, he offers me compassionate support. With his encouragement, I do go to work the following morning.

The minute I enter my office, the phone rings. It is Glenn, desperate to see me. "I'm parked just down the hill from the Courthouse. Please come down and meet me. We need to talk." I had probably just driven past him! Freaked out, I immediately report his location to the Sheriff. He is arrested soon thereafter. The die is cast.

Once I am assured that Glenn is locked up, a co-worker takes me to the Emergency Room to have my wounds looked at. And, in this small town, what should we find but several cops, already there with Glenn, who faked a heart attack when he was arrested. The nurses hide me in a back room until he is cleared and taken back to the jail.

That pivotal Monday, the clear choice to stand up for myself changed everything. The Universe works in remarkable ways to show us the path we must take. My daughter and her unborn child required me to be strong, and therefore I required it of myself.

That was the day I became a Feisty Woman, as I found my way to courage, to stand against anger, to say "no" once and for all to unacceptable behavior.

It was ironic: I had been a mental health professional for thirty years. How could this happen to me?

The lesson: no matter how smart and savvy we think we are, abuse and mistreatment of women occurs in every country and in every strata of society. It is up to each of us to stand for the respect that every woman deserves.

NOW WHAT?

How was I to cope with this startling new reality? It was August and I was not scheduled to retire until January. I couldn't live in my own house for several months. With blood spattered all over the bedroom, there was no longer any sense of safety and sanctuary there.

Fortunately, some dear friends offered me their mother-in-law flat, complete with a gorgeous pool and view in a gated community.

I still didn't feel safe. There were many subsequent Mondays when I called the Sheriff's Department, just to confirm that Mr. Bell was, in fact, still incarcerated.

The day of the trial came. Sierra had arrived from Colombia and her father Tom came from Northern California. Bolstered by their supportive presence, I found the strength to take the stand and testify against Glenn.

When he was brought into the courtroom (in an orange jumpsuit and chains), he immediately saw me surrounded by my family. Rather than looking contrite, he glared at me, mouthing "Shame!" as though it was my fault he was where he was.

Any shame I felt transformed into determination.

At this felony hearing, when I was asked why I didn't just run from him in Sonoma, all I could think was that the trauma had completely destroyed my power and agency. My fear of him paralyzed me. However, a fledgling Feisty spirit awoke the day I remembered in my brain fog that I had a camera on my phone. When Glenn went to the grocery store, I took some selfies of my wounds.

Those photographs and an ambitious female Prosecuting Attorney made sure that the Judge ordered this abuser to prison for five years.

So what was I meant to learn from this traumatic experience? My therapist Tamara urged me to begin by processing the trauma...

THE PREVIOUS MONDAY

Here is what occurred exactly one week before the choice-point Monday I just described.

At 3 am, I awoke to my estranged husband, backlit in my bedroom doorway.

"What are you doing here?" I gasped, "There is a restraining order against you!" He was supposed to be in his home in Sonoma, two hours away, not looming above me with a club of oak firewood.

Saying nothing, he immediately attacked, beating me savagely with the club as I tried to yell for help. But there was little chance of anyone hearing me on our isolated country property; the sound was more like the silent scream of a nightmare. Our caretaker Rob was no help; he lived in a trailer on the far side of the barn where he wouldn't hear me. Besides, he was as afraid of Glenn as I was.

Somehow I got the bedside light on to see blood spattered everywhere. He then took a small pistol out of the pocket of his sweatshirt and said, "I am a dead man so I might as well take you with me."

I will never know why he referred to himself as a dead man. It was either that he had recently been diagnosed with prostate cancer, or just knowing that he could go back to jail for breaking the restraining order to beat me bloody. In any case, I was sure that day would witness a murder/suicide and prepared to die.

Time seemed to stand still. Eventually after uncounted elongated moments, he put the gun away.

The next thing I remember is him ordering me to "clean this mess up; can't have anybody seeing all this blood."

He then demanded that I clean myself up. While I showered, he stood in the bathroom, watching, threateningly beating the club against his palm. He was making sure I couldn't reach the telephone.

Once I was dressed, he ordered me to make coffee and to call Rob. "Tell him Glenn is here but it's OK. Tell him not to call the police." I was numb with fear, and did as he asked.

Over coffee, he explained that he had hit me because he was afraid I would have Mace at my bedside, and he was mad that I had left him with no money. I responded that I expected him to live on his credit card, which I had always paid.

We talked more, but I was in shock and don't remember the content.

It was getting light, so I said, "Ok, I have to go to work."

He replied, "Oh no. If anyone sees you like this, I'll be arrested again. You're going with me to Sonoma."

On his orders, I contacted my office to say I would be away for a week due to a "family emergency." He was abducting me.

To be hit was shocking for me. I come from a loving family that never used any physical discipline. And my two former marriages were to gentle, caring men who never lifted a hand against me. I had no experience with the need for self-protection or fighting back. Even if I had known where the gun was, I would have no idea what to do with it. So I went with him.

He refused to take me to a hospital, but when we got to Sonoma, he applied some first aid to my wounds and ice to my swollen hand. He immediately began telling me how much he loved me and that he wanted to marry me again.

This was completely irrational. In the first place, we were still married; in the second, he had just nearly killed me. All I could do was lie in bed and wait for my wounds to heal. He kept insisting that we reconcile.

As the days went by and I began to feel a little better, he said, "I'm taking you to the ocean today."

In the past whenever we were in Sonoma and I suggested we go to the ocean he usually refused. But now he was trying to woo me, to placate me in order to get back into my good graces. I imagine that he was beginning to see what his life would be without my income.

He bombarded me with kindness and pressured me until I agreed to lift the restraining order and stop the divorce. It was the only way I could get him to take me home.

Sunday night, he brought me back. Mercifully, he then left, knowing he had to honor the restraining order until it was reversed.

HOW DID I GET HERE?

Tamara further encouraged me to consider how my choices had led to this experience.

Strangely, this journey began on September 11, 2001. When I contemplated those desperate people in the burning buildings calling their loved ones, I wondered: were I in that situation, who would I call?

I was 59, had been dating, but not seriously attached, for many years. It was a time in life when one choice would have been to relish my freedom.

In the last stage of life, the ancient people of India renounced the outer world, became wandering yogis, and retired to the forest to deepen their spiritual practice. While I had always been attracted to this plan for one's old age, my Inner Romantic still longed for the One Great Love. So 9/11 led me to Match.com. Don't laugh!

Glenn was handsome, sexy, smart, educated, a former athlete who won me over with his silver tongue. He told me he had searched the world wide web, and of all the women in the world, I was the one for him. How could I resist a line like that?

I ignored the fact that he had retired from teaching and directing fine art galleries and therefore had no money; his only asset was a house in Sedona which we sold to help finance our country property. Clearly, my desire for love blinded me to any financial concerns.

We were happy together for ten years. I was the breadwinner, he the house-husband, dog whisperer, passionate cook and resident artist.

But by year twelve, when his spending on sailboats, pedigree dogs, cars, and antique trucks veered out of control, I objected. He considered himself an Alpha Male and believed that the Natural Order required the woman to be led by the man (and therefore the woman was supposed to meekly accept the man's actions without objection.)

By then I held two jobs, working full-time as Family Court Services Director at the County Court and part-time with my private psychotherapy practice. I was also in my early 70's, was tired and ready to retire. He wouldn't hear me, and kept insisting that I work a few more years. My resentment fueled a break in our intimate life, which made him even angrier. He asked for a divorce.

While at first devastated, in time I accepted our situation and tried to discuss an equitable settlement. He stonewalled, refusing to make plans. Due to his profligate spending and unwillingness to negotiate a fair divorce settlement, I took his name off our bank accounts. Because I had always handled our finances and paid his credit card, he didn't even notice.

However, while I was visiting my daughter in South America, he discovered that he no longer had bank access and, when I returned, he was livid and dangerous. His behavior became so threatening that I was afraid to come home from work each evening. I asked him to move out of the house into his man-cave/artist studio in the barn.

He would alternatively agree and then trample those boundaries, coming into the house at all hours and especially into the bedroom, even when I had the door closed. When I threatened to lock the door, he retorted that he would just break it down.

The first time he hit me was a strong smack to the back of my head when I rejected an amorous approach.

From the beginning of our relationship, I had declared that any physical abuse would be a deal-breaker.

I called the police, intending only to register the event, not knowing about the California law requiring an investigation of every domestic violence call and the arrest of one of the parties.

The police came, he was arrested, and a restraining order was issued.

In May he moved to our get-away place in Sonoma two hours away. I relaxed, anticipating a prolonged divorce settlement dispute.

He had been gone for two months when, on that early morning in late July, he attacked me. He was not on drugs or alcohol. His actions seemed completely fueled by desperation, anger, and the dawning recognition that he could no longer control me. However, his deteriorating mental state may have been a result of dementia or other mental illness. I will never know. He served his five-year sentence, and there has been no contact since his release.

This is an OLD STORY. I am tired of it. Today I am letting it go.

The old paradigm (taught by my Mother) of "find a man to take care of you" has been replaced by an evolution of consciousness toward a vision of Woman, Free to be Herself.

I am still alive. I am very grateful for my freedom and a new life in a new country. I have lived near my daughter and granddaughter for almost seven years now, trading my roles of wife and professional woman for Mother and Grandmother.

Thankfully, my Inner Romantic has faded away (having learned her lesson the hard way). I now happily embody the Wise Woman/ Crone/ Renunciate Yogini.

Now I celebrate each Monday.

Every day is a new day.

About the Author

Mimi Rich holds a Master's Degree in Counseling Psychology and has practiced over thirty years as a psychotherapist in Massachusetts, California and now in Colombia.

https://linktr.ee/MimiRich

THE ULTIMATE SACRIFICE

BY POET KHAN RASS FIYAA

*"Educa a una Mujer y
Educates una nación."*

— MARCUS
GARVEY

Motherhood
is fetching water for your young from an impossible well,
everyday,
might as well be blind folded, hopefully blinded by the sun
but if blinded by the truth,
motherhood is choosing to walk in the dark.
Appropriately approaching an ocean so vast it is out of our grasp,
this bucket will never out last the weight of this present-day task
but… I'll try, I will try. Motherhood
is choosing to do something that someone else said they could
not do,
would say they are glad they did not do, in your face, somehow
respond with a smile.
Singular people tend to peer at us mysteriously, seemly fitting
because,
we have absolutely no idea what we are doing as parents. None.
Left with the physical, spiritual, mental, ramifications of
watching your being decay to bring forth life, healing that episiotomy.
Motherhood
is having your reality taken off the shelf, thrown down the cellar
towers of doom.
Your closest friends in a zoom room, pathetic and trying not to be,
just broken, empty.
It was one good night now; it is for life.
It was supposed to be a picket fence and an F-150
or a Toyota Corolla and a condo in The Downtown Artists District,
it was supposed to be a 2-car garage on the outskirts of the city or
at least a fucking check to expect each month.
My experience with fatherhood crumbled to silence on both
occasions.
Motherhood
is blaming yourself for your fuck up, rightfully so.
But also blaming yourself for the outcome of someone else's life,
someone that knows you are desperate for the kind of support only
they could supply, and they simply cannot give it to you.

We know that we are not capable at times,
Sometimes, more than others this is true.
Some mothers were robbed of their innocence becoming robbers of
the innocent.
Have not been allotted the time nor space to admit what happened.
Some of us function from a time warp.
We tell ourselves one day, someday, while blowing our potential in a
cloud of haze,
purple preferably.
We need support as women.
It has nothing to do with being independent, we need a second
opinion, need hands that grab ass, grab that baby bag, the groceries,
grab my spirit when I forget I am the prize King.
Take her with you for your time with the fellas because I need a
chance to reset this segment.
Motherhood
is needing a break like you need the veins in your body to allow DNA
to cascade through, coding who you are, remembering that you used
to be more than a mommie
somewhere in you, still more than just a mommie.
Crying yourself to sleep,
crying yourself awake
keeping a cloud of haze all day just like your mother did.
Single Motherhood
Is hoping your fatherless sons turn out better.

Motherhood is a phenomenon, but being a single mother
warrants a class of its own.

There is a chance she was raised by a single mother,
spent her entire childhood saying she would be better, that she would
never be a single mother. To wake up one day and realize that both of
your kids know the same pain that you felt, the difference is that they
lack representation.

I cannot describe the waves of guilt that I consume daily. Looking at them, feeling I robbed them of something they need almost more than me.

I chose someone that could not give them stability, just like my mother did. Except, they are boys, seeking a man, with a penis. I remember my son asking me mommie, what is it for? What is this thing? I hung my head and waited for the imaginary dad to walk through the door only to raise my head and meet my budding preteen's eyes. Looking at me for answers on manhood, black manhood, black manhood in America.

How do you teach your children that they are the most wanted?

I had to come to the understanding that their fathers gave me the best of themselves.

What is healing? Why would the mother need to heal? Broken mothers make broken daughters which make broken homes destroying the nation slowly, a dripping faucet.

The woman destroys her home, the mother destroys the lineage.

Healing is facing that which hurts you and forgiving yourself and others. If she does not, she will spew and attract the same hurt.

I recently made the decision to rid myself of my mother's grief. Sometimes a mother's healing is removing herself from the first person that taught her love, because love was demonstrated as pain. I realize I seek pain in all my relationships because pain was love, abandonment, a form of control.

Today I am finding what the sun feels like without my mother in this world. It's learning how to walk again. My community embraces me thankfully; I lack nothing. Do whatever it takes to heal, sever any relationship that keeps you from peace. You deserve it. You are the change.

I lived in the La Armada housing projects in my hometown of Corpus Christi for 4 years with my two boys. No one should live in detrimental circumstances and be expected to have some kind of pride in being a mother. The low rent is matched with the low morale that slowly turns into depression that you numb with a habit you cannot afford, but somehow do. Rat droppings, a refrigerator infested with roaches.

The government assistance, welfare system, prison system, all of it is set up to destroy black families.

Black families need fathers, just as much as any other culture does. He is vital to its survival. Young boys watch their mothers struggle to keep the lights on and food on the table, they see how the overpowering lack affects her, and because they love their mother and see that no one else is here to help as she combats her own mental health as well, they find a way, make a way. Love tends to do that.

Poverty is a structure that is designed to keep us from experiencing the American dream. Considering the location, the Projects, or any other poverty-stricken circumstance, most young boys turn to what is accessible to them: drugs. Before they are 20, they have been caught by the police at least once, and hopefully they do not seek solace in their own supply. But eventually, most do. The black young man is free just long enough to get a young woman pregnant, and there is the cycle as planned.

I realized that experiencing abundance in life was more than just fixing my credit and getting a better job. I had to heal, I had to heal to become rich, heal physically, emotionally and spiritually. I had to heal in order to attract opulence. Without the cleaning of the house, money was always going to be in want.

This chapter is my penance to motherhood and the sacrifices I have made to keep my 2 boys safe, even from their fathers.

I remember the day I found out I was pregnant. The day I told his father. The day I held Isaiah in my arms. He was so proud to be mine, he knew I would do whatever I could to protect him. His smile said so. He still has that same smile: that hero smile. I tell him often that he has his father's smile.

Somehow, I never lost the beauty in the possibility of us. It would be outweighed by a heavier weight of grief, another baby father leaving me. Magically I strive, but this year I realized: I have been in survival mode for the last decade. A decade of being run by poverty, doing only what I can afford, cannot afford to want.

The thing is, I was a broken person before my children. More so crippled by a debilitating lack of self-confidence. Everything I pursued—love, friendships, relationships, business opportunities, eating better—all of it was attempted with a lack of faith in myself.

Furthermore, I twirled the same excuses over and over for years. I watched other people, have things I did not believe for myself, these things that I begged on the inside for, but also told myself it would never happen, thereby neutralizing my desire. The result? The same results, repeatedly.

The horrifying thing about motherhood is: if you do not face your demons, traumas, the incidents that happen to you that you do not even remember because you chose to protect yourself from them, they will continue to resurface. You have heard this a million times, here is a million and one: it's true.

My oldest son's dad was on crack. Hard to admit, but he was already gone when I met him. He was so beautiful. I met his mother first, on her deathbed, dying of lung cancer. She loved her son, showed me a picture of him, and honestly, I fell in love with him right then. He was in jail at that moment.

The first time I laid eyes on him was at her funeral. I remember him fainting at her coffin side. They loved each other so dearly. Fred was gone before he even had the chance to be a dad. Two daughters he was no longer able to see; he always wanted a son.

He grew up within the heart of drugs' influence. Even a beautiful 24-year-old black young woman pregnant with his baby, his first son, was not pronounced enough. Never thought I would have a baby by a person that eventually I would have to give up on.

Living with him in Austin Texas while 6 months pregnant, I didn't know I was amongst crack heads and junkies, thieves, con artists. Didn't know I had fallen in love with one. I remember the smell of burning plastic and bleach. The way Fred would try to keep a straight face after he came back from the neighbor's house. "Preacher" was his name. He was a good man, just trapped by the effects of poverty.

I moved back to Corpus Christi, TX so I could have the baby near my family. I got an apartment, paid the rent with my unemployment. All he had to do was come home and take care of me. I lost everything. This gorgeous baby with cowlicks I would rather say came from my father instead of his father. My best friend at the time was my lover. She carried me. She was ashamed of our sessions of nipple sucking and blunt passing, she hoped God did not see us, but, she was my savior.

I moved to El Paso with my mother. Long story short, it took me years to come to the conclusion of what me and Fred were and why? He had on the inmate prison boxers when I met him, and he never took them off. I remember looking his name up to see if he was in jail one random day, and he was. I knew then I'd made the right decision by leaving him, even though I didn't want to. He gave me the best of himself: my beautiful, charming, loving Isaiah.

It took me 10 years to be completely grateful for his blessing, wholeheartedly, because he has the chance to live a good life. I have the power to give him that chance. Sometimes, that is accomplished by leaving the other parent.

DJ was my distant lover. Dark skin, an eye for fashion, rapper, and knew how to dominate in the bedroom in a way that had me addicted. When he was free, he spent a lot of time avoiding me. At first it was because of his mother. He was so close to his mother. I learned from my first boyfriend James to not date a man that hates his mother; he will hate you, too.

One year older than me, DJ was from Georgia. I walked up to him and a group of his friends looking for some recreational activities, he reached out and grabbed my hand. He fell in love with me at first sight.

He was always so confident. It would destroy him in the end. We both were sex addicts, were both robbed at a young age sexually, both people pleasers that were capable of having ground shaking, super boles of pleasure. Kismet when we met. He satiated me.

When I found out I was pregnant with Jordan, I had just had a "lets try again" with Fred, so I thought the baby was Fred's. But there was something about the way DJ responded when I told him; he had traces of joy in his tone. I was too afraid of being rejected again to try to see if DJ wanted to be a dad, so I told him the baby was Fred's.

Jordan was born the year after I survived being stabbed by a then-lover in 2013. I held the most beautiful bundle of joy with his big, juicy, full lips. I should have known he was DJ's, he kept telling me he wanted to get Jordan tested to confirm paternity, even though he was light-skinned. I let Jordan's light skin be my scapegoat, and I was so wrong.

DJ was a truck driver, and his mother died suddenly while scuba diving, leaving him 50 grand to miss her with. He was so broken, he stayed away from me, but he sent me money whenever I needed it while he could.

After I had Isaiah, I wrote a letter to Fred while in jail telling him, a secret, the secret, my secret. He called me 2 weeks after Isaiah's birth to tell me he was done with me, he did not want someone who had a disease and had someone else.

There was no way in hell I was going to trust someone else with my deepest truth, so I kept pushing DJ away to avoid having to be that vulnerable with him.

Looking back, he loved me, and he may have stepped up to being a father had I really made room for it.

Dark chocolate skin gave me a baby boy whose skin is lighter than mine. He came out clapping and may end up being the next John Legend or Barack Obama. His confidence in himself is innate, teleported straight to him from his father.

It would be after DJ received 2 life sentences for a rape he says he did not commit, that he would finally tell me Jordan was his, topping it off with a tattoo of his name on his back. The amount of pain and regret I felt.

The last time I saw DJ, Jordan was laying next to us as we squeezed in a quickie. He wanted to come back home with me, and I did not let him. I wanted to keep a roommate comfortable, not knowing she already had plans of comfort of her own, still comfortably married to this day. The amount of regret I felt and feel sometimes.

I wrote a book about him to help me process never having him in my life, my arms, my vagina again. My beautiful Jordan will never get to see his daddy free, there are no strokes on this keyboard for that. I consider if God took them both because I would have never given up.

Especially on DJ, I was so in love with him. I waited for him for a while and then realized I had to move on, it was hell telling him too but it had to be done.

Motherhood is knowing that the father's current situation is not worthy of your son, and letting that be your tissue on nights where it's nothing but why coming through the speakers.

Our young boys love us like no other: pure, innocent love. When the mother is too broken to be present in the day-to-day emotional support of her children, the child is left to rot in a world of shadows. Constantly needing, seeking someone's approval and attracting people to them that they must constantly prove love to.

Narcissistic mothers never see their children as worthy of apologies, no matter the circumstance. These women raise young women with low self-esteem and boys who are ego-stricken. There are mothers who hate their children because they hate themselves and will never choose to heal; they destroy this house from the inside out.

Motherhood is facing the very aspects of yourself, the trauma bonds formed to function in a society that hates you, will never stop hating you and your fatherless black sons. A moon with no sun, a child without his mother's love, there is no orbit to be spun.

No jokes, no puns, the punchline is the dust on this child support card. One year he paid, out of 11 years.

Motherhood is finding the light in that.

It is watching innocent people drown because you could not save them, and you were the only one that could.

As a single mother, we must take on the task of addressing and healing ourselves so we can live the best lives possible. Our loved ones suffer everyday that we do not live our full potential.

Give yourself and your loved ones the best you by doing the necessary shadow work. You are so worth it.

About the Author

She is becoming...

Born in the Gulf of Mexico, now residing in the El Paso Texas desert, a mother of two Suns. A voice for prison reform, a mental health advocate, as well as a pleasure poet pursuing her first dream of creating unconquerable spaces for vulnerability and sensuality in the poetic world.

A King Maker, Queen Mentor, advocate of compassion and love. A co-host of The Grape Vine Sway LLC open mic hosting a Tuesday night show, as well as co-host of the award winning El Paso Barb Wire Open Mic Series which airs every Monday. Also, a member of The Word is Write platform where she cohost a sensual show, Moist Mondays. She is the published author of " CPR to My Dreams (An Ode to 2020)"& "My Abyss"(I wrote him free), a poetic depiction of incarcerated love.

She has works included in 5 anthologies including "Salute to Black Women" and "Salute to Black Men" poetry collection as well as "Global Poets Drop the Mic" anthology.

Her most recent publication is in, Life In The Times, a Border Senses project in response to living in a pandemic. She is Love, Peace and Light, pursuing abundance.

https://linktr.ee/Poetkhan

THE TRUTH HAS TEETH

BY SIERRA MELCHER

I walk in the rain. Not because it's poetic or romantic. I walk in the rain because I fucking hate umbrellas.

We are each a unique concoction of what we were born with & our lived experience. Sharing the specifics of my trauma here will not heal me at this moment & knowing the specifics won't heal you either. In fact, it runs the risk of retraumatizing you. So I won't.

Suffice it to say, I lost my voice one day at the end of a dirt road. I was no more than six.

My silence settled in.

There's a lot of things I don't remember but I remember that goddamn umbrella. Maybe it's still on the side of that road.

I learned I wasn't safe in a girl's body. And that my voice wasn't enough. Because I used it that day, and it didn't protect me. So I stopped.

That's the day I learned that my voice wasn't enough to keep me safe. That's the day I learned to be quiet and pretend everything was fine.

I have very distinct memories as a young girl of lying. I started lying about everything: where I was, if I went to school or not, what I ate, who I was with, what I wanted, who I was. Lying was the perfect pass to appear "good" and easily-approved-of without having to either do better, or risk disappointment, disapproval, and even punishment.

For a long time, despite the pain, it felt safer to lie.

Growing up, I couldn't cry. Anytime I flooded with emotions it felt like someone was standing on my throat. I wondered if I would suffocate under the pressure. I couldn't breathe. I couldn't swallow. I couldn't speak the truth. My words and feelings were tightly bottled up and stored in my chest, locked in my throat.

I learned the silence of survival. I started to feel like I didn't exist, because I was faking everything.

Becoming a mother transformed so many things for me. My daughter Eden was born feisty. I see it as my job to make sure she stays that way. She is six now, the age I was that day on the side of the road. I am nervous for her. It's re-triggering watching my young girl wear a dress. The part of me that was not protected that day is hyper-vigilant and overprotective of her.

Sometimes she's more the teacher than I because she hasn't had a silence instilled in her. She is helping me rediscover my feisty, not the other way around.

When it comes to communication, I obviously am quite attentive to preserving her voice. Ironically, expression is not a struggle for her. With the focused intention of supporting her to communicate, we normalize discussing the uncomfortable or frustrating things, to feel safe speaking the truth without fear of retribution or rejection, to create conscious and intentional spaces. We practice hard conversations. We make this the norm... and who is learning more here?

Being feisty is about breaking out of the acceptable norm, not allowing others to dictate who we are and *how* we are. Rather, really taking the time and knowing that it is valuable, worthy, for us to discover who we are. For us to more fully step into that expression of ourselves. That is where we are healthy. That is where we are true. That is where we are most potent and impactful.

For anyone who's ever faked it, we know how isolating that feels. If you're accepted but you know you're faking it, it doesn't feel like true acceptance. If you're hiding who you really are, it doesn't feel like anyone really sees you. If you're holding back, it doesn't feel like anyone really understands you. When we're faking it, it is so lonely and so exhausting.

To be ourselves, to be feisty takes energy and courage. When we can be, the rewards of being seen and heard and held and accepted and loved as we are—raw, imperfect, truthful, and occasionally a mess—is the most delicious feeling.

When we can write from this place of truth, from our own authentic reality, when we can bravely transmute our voice onto the page, the question is no longer, "What if I can't?" Rather, the question becomes, "What else can I do?"

A few years ago, I received a strange kind of gift for my birthday: a transformational experience that simultaneously exposed the core and deep awareness of my trauma, and delivered the antidote to my silence.

The Truth Has Teeth.

What I didn't realize was that my silence was still hurting me. That I was continuing to play out the consequences of something that had happened 35+ years earlier. I was carrying the impact of that day into the present.

So many times
I did not say what I wanted
Did not ask for what I needed
Pretended everything was fine
Gripped in the silence that was born that day.
The simplest thing is to speak the truth.

That was the thing I had to do, the simplest: just open my mouth and tell the people that I care about how I feel. I still stumble here.

Knowing with more clarity the root cause helped me rediscover the comfort and the safety I was born with. I have learned to cry. I have learned to use my voice in all of its iterations: out loud and in the written word, sometimes preferring the safety of the page.

Which is more challenging for you: speaking out loud, or writing your heart out?

When it comes to writing, since we run a publishing company, we help women write and publish their books so that they can become leaders in their fields and change the world, by offering world-class support, coaching & courses at every stage of the author process. This element of finding your voice and fiercely holding your feisty, is quintessential. It is the prerequisite.

Through the practice of writing, women in our community rediscover their voices. But it is impossible to write and publish if we feel silenced within ourselves. For this reason, it is so important to me that we do more than just publish books. Women have this inherent power. But one of the crippling effects of having grown up in the world is that many of us have lost or been disconnected, have forgotten that we have this magnificent creative force in the shape of our own voice, our own expression. This is partly why writing is so powerful, and why it is so transformative. It is through the digesting of and reflecting on our own experiences that we can heal our stories. We can teach others. We can give permission to countless others by being willing to sit in our own experience and to navigate and explore the capacity of our own voices.

To me, feisty is the fluid and fierce claiming of our own voices, our own selves, as we are. With none of the bullshit, or the trying or the pretending to be something else.

When I started this I would say, "The world needs more feisty women." It's not so much that. We're all plenty feisty. However, we don't realize it. We don't realize how feisty we are. I spent the bulk of my life silenced and self-editing.

In writing this chapter, I realized that even though it's taken me years, I've always been feisty, even in my silence, even in my faking it.

Here's my *Feisty* list:

- In high school, I ran for student body president and lost all three times.
- I moved across the country to go to university.
- I drove across the USA in an old beat-up car.
- In college, I applied for a leadership job because I was shy & discovered I was good at it.

- After graduating, I traveled to Europe alone because travel terrified me & I discovered what I am capable of.
- I moved to San Francisco on a hunch and drove 3300 miles alone.
- I became a teacher because I was a terrible student & discovered I loved it.
- I shaved my head twice & dyed leopard print on my head.
- I go to restaurants and ask the waiter to bring me anything; "Surprise me."
- I moved to China, twice.
- I bought goats because I wanted to make chevre (goat's cheese).
- I took a job and moved to Colombia with seven days notice.
- I traveled for love countless times. Never finding what I was after. But finding something amazing anyway.
- I quit my job with no plan in place.
- I opened a yoga studio while seven months pregnant.
- I broke up with my boyfriend at eight months pregnant.
- I gave birth at home.
- Every problem I solved; sometimes creating new ones, but solving those problems too.
- I wrote books, lots of books.
- I opened a publishing company.
- I hired people before I knew where the money was coming from.
- I bought a banjo that I still can't play, just to piss off the neighbors.
- I learned to speak Spanish despite my dyslexia.
- I bought a car and even land in a foreign country, again and again.
- I did things that I didn't know I knew how to do. But I did them anyway. And I have ever learned or confirmed that I already know.

My list can go on and on.

And it should. And it will, never fear.

But if I can offer you one thing in this chapter, it is my hope that you will make *your own* feisty list.

I think the truth is: we all have stories. Experiences that hammers in what's taught us: to behave, to smile, to play right, to be pretty, to not make a fuss. My story reminds me that I am so much more than what has happened to me.

I showed you my list. Now make yours:

What makes you FEISTY? How and when and where have you been bold too? Shown much courage, been ridiculous and fully yourself?

- I am feisty because ___
- I am feisty when ___
- I have been feisty by ___

Share this list. Inspire and encourage others.

I am the choices I get to make each and every day. I am the opportunity to be more silly, more ridiculous. Braver, bolder, kinder, more generous, more supportive & more grateful.

It's no accident that I run an all-female publishing company supporting women to find their voices, write their stories, and become thought leaders who change the world. I know well what it feels like to be separated from my voice. I'm not having any more of it. Not for me, and not for you. We all still have choices. We also have the opportunity: our voice. It's just a matter of whether or not we choose to use it.

To all the feisty women, all the feisty girls, all the feisty people the world over: Thank you for being yourself! Thank you for not shrinking into any size box. Thank you for your weird. Thank you for taking the time to figure out who you are, what lights you up, and how to be you. The world needs more of you. Thank you.

About the Author

Best-selling author, international speaker & educator, Sierra Melcher is founder of **Red Thread Publishing LLC.**, an all-female publishing company to help women write & publish their books so that they can become leaders in their fields & change the world, by offering world-class support, coaching & courses at every stage of the author process. Writing & Publishing intentionally accelerates personal, spiritual & professional growth. BECAUSE EVERY STORY MATTERS.

Sierra has a Master's degree in education, has spoken & taught around the world. Originally from the United States, Sierra lives in Medellin, Colombia with her young daughter.

If you are interested in writing or publishing with us, reach out: https://linktr.ee/redthreadpublishing

RESETTING FAMILY HISTORY

HOW THE POWER OF OUR VOICE CAN BREAK
GENERATIONAL BONDS

BY BRANDEE MELCHER

Somewhere along the way, the women in my family were told to settle and accept life for what it is. Unfortunately, they came to believe this lie and worse, this lie was passed along as an irrefutable fact to every girl in my family. Each of us believed this ornately dressed up piece of fiction, including myself, until I decided I'd had enough and called the police on my father for the first time, at the age of eleven.

I am the great-granddaughter of Helen Minerva Vincent (Mikola). A first generation Finnish-American citizen who came of age in Northern Michigan prior to the passage of the 19th amendment in 1919. A woman dripping with eight children who was dependent upon an abusive, alcoholic husband. A husband and father who would send his fourth daughter, Dolores June Edgington, to live on her own at the young age of eleven simply because she asked her father to stop drinking and stop the physical, emotional and mental abuse he freely shared.

Dolores June Edginton (Vincent), my Nana, born June 3, 1938, came into this world full of moxie and grit, which would serve her well as she found herself financially responsible for her life because she dared to speak up. Unfortunately, all of the financial freedoms—

personal bank account, private apartment and owning a vehicle—she worked hard for since childhood would not allow her entry into college and would be traded for supposed marital bliss and a life-long partner.

My Pappaw, who has been sober for over 40 years, hardly provided the financial security my Nana had traded in the name of love. In fact, he would later give consent for my mother's under-age marriage in 1984 in an attempt to avoid potential child-support payments.

At 10:25 am on August 7, 1985, Toni Lynn Burke (Edgington) at the age of 17, found herself mother to a brand new human, and a military wife to someone she had known for approximately a year. Fear, hope, anxiety, self-doubt and joy would form the foundation of my childhood as we traveled to Colorado to begin our new life.

My mother quickly discovered that solitude was her closest friend as she raised a child far from the comforts of Maryland. Away from the safety net she didn't know she needed, Toni found herself naked on a balcony on a snowy winter night with no jacket, socks, shoes or under garments—saved from spending the night on the balcony by a neighbor who happened to look out, noticed her, and called the police.

This was far from happily ever after, and yet uncomfortably familiar to the life she had known growing up. Despite the harsh reality of her marriage, Toni stayed married, as there were not many options for a single teenage mother in the late 1980's.

As I grew, my mother tried to pass along the few life lessons she had been handed: *be quiet, life happens to you not for you, accept all and question little.* I was motivated to buck the system early, frequently grounded and physically punished for being *sassy, outspoken and bitchy.*

One of my proudest punishments came at the age of nine when my parents questioned me and demanded to know what gave me the right to act and say the things I did—which was mainly calling bullshit on the double standards set for me—and I proudly answered, *"The Declaration of Independence grants all people life, liberty and the pursuit of happiness with free speech."*

Needless to say, that answer was not well received.

Two short years later, we found ourselves on a quiet cul-de-sac in the middle of suburbia in a neighborhood that had kids in almost every house. It was an ideal place to raise a family. The cul-de-sac served as a kickball / softball field / basketball court, with our front yard acting as an extension of home base for flashlight tag, and a grassy field for flag football when we needed somewhere a little softer to land.

It was also the perfect location with plenty of room for three police cars to pull up that fateful evening.

The fight began as it always did: snarky comments here, voices raised there, deep cutting insults, and the past being dredged up from the depths. As the war between our parents raged and the fighting moved to the upstairs bedroom, I had had enough. I watched as my younger brother made himself small in the living room while watching TV, and my youngest brother crawled up the stairs in pursuit to stop the chaos. I didn't stop him this time. I thought he may actually be able to put a stop to it for the evening. Instead, he nearly lost his life.

The yelling intensified and for some reason, the thought of calling the 911 emergency line came to me. It had never occured to me before, but I needed help, and knew this was the only way. The phone felt heavy in my small hand as I listened intently to the noises upstairs, waiting for the operator to pick up.

Then there was a woman on the line, asking me:

What was the emergency?

What did I need?

Were there weapons in the house?

What was my name?

How old was I?

Were there any other children in the house?

I explained the best I could as to what was happening, who was here, and asking for the police to please show up quickly, as I heard a large crash, my mother scream, and now silence. I would later learn that the crash was my mother's dresser being toppled to the ground and my mother screaming as she saved my youngest brother from being crushed.

I could hear both voices and footsteps. I explained to the operator that I needed to hang up now because I had nowhere to hide and still talk—a corded phone in the middle of the family kitchen allowed no hiding places—so I pushed the button, and the line went dead.

One thing I didn't know was: when you hang up on the police, they call back.

Panic set in as I heard the phone ring, because I knew who it was. I had to answer before my father could, so I did. I quickly said "I'm okay, just please send help," and I hung up again.

My father was down the steps sooner than I had anticipated: he knew the phone had been answered. I did the best I could to put as much space as possible between him and myself. He screamed at me, wanting to know who had called. I was paralyzed. I couldn't answer, because I knew it would not end well for me if he knew the police were coming.

As he was yelling and hitting me for answering the phone, it started ringing again. It wouldn't stop. I just needed the ringing to stop and I would be safe. And it did... when he answered.

The rageful fear that consumed his face as he spoke to the operator was a turning point for me. Initially, I was terrified, because I had never seen that expression before, and yet...

And yet, I felt an inner calm begin to form. I had found *the thing* that could potentially keep me and my family safe from my father.

The operator asked to speak with me. He threw the phone in my direction, scrambling to leave the house before the police showed up.

That night was the first time I reached out for help. While the help was slow and imperfect in showing up, it came. I learned that my voice, no matter how feeble and shaken it was that night, had the power to change our lives. I dared to share the secret no other woman in my family could tell, and I lived. I was bruised, swollen and sore, but I lived.

I cannot thank Little Brandee enough for finding her voice that night and for each night after that. She learned the power of words, her voice, and sharing long-held generational secrets. Little Brandee unknowingly shifted the course of history for every one of my descendants that night.

Today, I share with my daughters the power of using our voices. From knowing the importance of voting, having a private personal bank account, and speaking up for ourselves and others, my daughters will be encouraged to shape life *for* themselves and not simply accept it for what it is.

I am the woman my great grandmother could have never envisioned.

I am the woman my Nana always wanted to be.

I am the woman my mother feared.

I am the woman to reset my family's history

About The Author

Brandee Melcher coaches unmothered women, guiding them in unpacking their generational boxes of inherited lies. As a child that grew up witnessing domestic violence and a mother of two daughters, Brandee knows the importance of challenging the history you've been handed in order to create the future you and future generations deserve. Going on her own journey to reconnect with Little Brandee has brought her more inner peace and helped her become a more understanding parent. Brandee will help you unpack your boxes, find your inner magic, connect with Little You and reestablish boundaries that were lost to the traumas of life.

https://linktr.ee/brandeemelcher

RE-WRITING THE RULE BOOK

BY STEPHANIE GALINDO

T he first truly brave decision I ever made was part of my initiation into motherhood, in my second year of marriage. It's the first time that my deeper knowing was distinctly at odds with the authority structure around me, and the first time I made a decision to trust myself over and against the voices above me.

At the time, my husband, Michael, and I were living in a unique situation, where authority was everything. We had chosen together to join a movement where every element of our adult lives was determined by the same authority structure (the particular organization will remain unnamed for my own wellbeing). Our jobs, housing, education, retirement plans—even our furnishings, vehicles, computers, and childcare fund were all wrapped up in one tidy little package. Talk about having all your eggs in one basket!

We were in the schooling process for this career, which was even more overbearing than the career itself. We lived in a small apartment in a dormitory on campus where we had daily classes, mandatory after school responsibilities, weekend commitments, and practicums that replaced summer and Christmas breaks. One of our small group leaders would always say to the group at large, "Whatever you do, just don't get pregnant while you're here."

But just 3 months into our 2 years at this training school, and only 6 months into our marriage, I discovered that "just don't get pregnant" was not as easy for us as I had assumed it would be.

I remember crying on the phone with my mom when I found out I was pregnant because, even though I wanted kids, the negative stigma built up on campus was palpable. Having a brain that is extra sensitive to rejection, I heard every comment as if it were directed at me: gossip about previous students who got pregnant at school; that pregnancy was irresponsible; that at other similar schools, you would be kicked out for getting pregnant—even as a married couple!

We worked hard to keep up with the demands of this rigorous program, while also adding in the prenatal visits, hormone changes, and all of the decision-making that comes with planning for a new arrival.

But I always felt so uncomfortable leaving the doctor visits, because they felt manipulative and demeaning, and it didn't feel right to me. For example, every choice offered had the tone of "you can do A or B, but if you do B, your baby might have brain damage." Choices like whether to take every possible additional test regarding your own health or the health of your baby were so emotionally exhausting. Every time I said no to something that I had concluded was unnecessary, the response I received from nurses made me feel like I was being irresponsible.

"Am I irresponsible?" I would leave my appointments wondering. "Maybe I can't trust my own body, my own mind to guide me."

As the due date approached, I became more and more terrified.

I remember a moment of realization where I told Michael, "I just realized I'm not at all afraid of the birthing process itself. I'm afraid of the doctor, and the hospital, and the feeling that my care providers won't have my best interests in mind."

That spark of clarity made all the difference. Armed with that deeper knowing in my spirit, I started looking for alternatives to a hospital birth. I determined that what felt right for me was to be in the care of a midwife instead of a doctor. I found a homebirth midwife willing to take me even as late in the pregnancy as I already was. I met with her and felt so much better. All the fear I had melted away, and I gained confidence in my ability to safely birth the child I was carrying.

There was just one hiccup. She didn't practice out of a birth center, and only provided care for home births. Because of our tremendous trust in the institution at that time (read: naïveté), we opted to be fully transparent with our intentions and ask permission from the "powers-that-be" to have the baby there in our own apartment.

They discussed it.

We waited.

And they said no.

So we explored other options: hotel suites, other local birthing centers, nearby friend's houses (yeah… that's kind of a big ask). I continued exploring options as it became harder and harder to pick myself up off the floor (literally).

But then, my water broke 17 days early. After some frantic inquiries to explore any other last-minute options that came to mind, we headed home to meet the midwife in the comfort of our institutional apartment.

Ok, "comfort" might be an overstatement, at least for me. At that time in my life, I was not very well connected with my own body.

Translation: I was clueless.

Every moment of 36 long hours of pain, sweat, and back-labor felt never ending. There were times I truly believed I couldn't keep going. But there was never a time that I wished I were in the hospital. Never a moment that I regretted or questioned my choice. At the end of the day, I laid down in my own bed, with the handmade quilt from our wedding, baby Sammy in the crook of my arm, and Michael beside me.

Just a week after the baby was born, my body was beginning to recover, despite functioning on about 8 total hours of sleep in the whole week. Two high ranking officials scheduled a time to come meet with Michael and myself, inside of our own apartment. Reflecting back, I realize this was the first of many stiff communications during that season of life.

We were reprimanded and put on probation because of our choice to disregard their authority. Michael respectfully accepted the news, recognizing that it was the choice we made, which felt right to us regardless of the consequences. There was a sense of shock and relief from the leadership as they walked out the door. They had clearly been expecting excuses, defiance, or complaints, not to be met with confident, personal responsibility.

Samuel's birth story is my first radical moment of allowing my inner voice to outrank societal expectations.

For me, up until that point, I would have been a people-pleaser if I could have been. Call me a "people-pleaser wannabe." There was just something within me that never consented.

I sought external validation from a very young age, so I always cared what people thought, and wanted them to be happy. But even knowing they weren't happy didn't cause my behavior to bend to their preferences. It just caused me to carry, for years, the guilt of nonconformity. I possessed both a deep desire for approval as well as an immovable core that refused to bend or shift to the likings of others. I was the world's ambassador to my soul, begging it to make peace with the world's "supposed to be." I was supposed to be quieter, more respectful. I was supposed to get along with people and not say things that make them uncomfortable. I was supposed to have my baby off-campus. In a hospital. With doctors.

Being the liaison between society and my soul was a losing position. One filled with shame, failure, and non-congruence.

That being said, I did find ways to get my positive reinforcement. I spent my free time volunteering for youth programs, music programs, and teaching programs.

I had always done a lot of seemingly brave and independent things, but only those things that elicited applause from the voices of authority surrounding me, like service trips overseas, and teaching English high in the mountains of Honduras for over two years. But the first actually brave thing I ever did wasn't until years later, when I chose to trust my own voice above those in authority over me.

Shortly after Sammy was born, I took a drive to see some childhood friends. They were desperate to hear how my journey to motherhood was, and how I was doing. But I was so shaken up by the choice I had made that, initially, I felt this need to gush out every detail of our choice and defend it.

Their response was complete indifference to the institutional strain, pushing me into the natural communion of new moms. Essentially, they were saying, "Your bosses and their opinions mean nothing to us, tell us how you and the baby are doing." As obvious as that may sound, it came like a splash in the face. I didn't know yet how to stand behind my own choices, to have my own back.

A journey always starts somewhere. I'm so grateful that since that day, I have learned to have my own back, and to trust my choices. Learned to become my own cheerleader. What I've discovered along the way is that the deep self-acceptance that has come through that journey, has also transformed my relationships. I used to focus on how to show up to a relationship in a way that met the other person's expectations. Now I show up as my whole self, and that one shift has brought new people into my life. People who are aligned with me, accepting of me, and on the journey with me.

At the same time, it was also my relationships that transformed me, such as the role my husband played in this pivotal experience.

One question that often pops up in small discussions around Christmas time is the smallness of the role Joseph played in the ancient texts of the Holy Family. "Where was Joseph in this story?" the old pastors would ask with suspicion. His passive role is minimal. In my own story, I reflected on the same question, "Where was Michael in this story?"

The answer is the same: They both know when it's time to take a seat.

Michael didn't need to understand my perspective of birth and "get on board." He didn't feel entitled to a role in the decision-making process. He didn't demand a thorough explanation of my thought process. Him not questioning my own inner knowing was significant in my own ability to trust.

I only reflected back on this recently, when a pregnant friend mentioned to me that she wanted a planned C-section, but her husband wanted her to try for a vBac first. I was sincerely shocked. It never occurred to me that a man would have the audacity to have an opinion about that.

That conversation made me realize that unlike her experience, Michael never gave me the impression that it wasn't up to me. He never asked me to question my own voice.

Michael's trusting role in my life solidified my belief that relationships are a key ingredient to our transformation. When I look at the most pivotal moments in my life, they are all held in the container of relationship: from Michael's trust in me through my first birth story, to the influence of a particular coach who led me to believe that I could literally do anything, and ultimately empowered me with the bravery to launch the coaching practice I have today.

So while self-acceptance is the foundational pillar of my coaching, relationship is the container that holds it. Looking back, I see how these two principles were birthed right there, in that defiant first moment of motherhood.

I've come to discover that many others have journeys that started much like mine, whose 'feisty' had been trained out of them for years before that pivotal moment when they heard it calling them back.

Sammy's birth was my first brave step, and since then, being feisty has looked very different through the various stages of my life so far. Even in my current season of entrepreneurship, it's meaning has expanded several times.

Most recently, feisty has looked like fully embracing my soul's calling to relationship coaching within my neurodiverse community. It has called upon me to foster radical self acceptance in every person. For those of us who see ourselves as just a little outside the confines of social norms, we might run the hamster wheel for a while, trying to make it into the circle of societal expectations, always just out of reach. But eventually we wake up to an inner voice that can't be ignored, a voice that calls us to stop living by default, by the expectations of others, and by obligation, and start living by design, purpose, and a deep sense of internal satisfaction: to trust our own voice to lead us in the way that is right for us.

In a world of definitive societal expectations, choosing a different path for myself has caused discomfort, uncertainty, and even vulnerability. But I wouldn't have it any other way. Because listening to my own inner voice has also brought my soul freedom, peace, and an openness to life I hadn't imagined possible.

I believe that you also have a voice within you, calling you to live in congruence with your own self.

Can you hear it?

Can you separate it from the voices of authority, of societal expectation, and of obligation?

A recent client of mine, Amy, came to me initially wanting a coach to help force her to be more productive. She assumed that more productivity was what was missing in her life. Through coaching, we discovered that the voice that always told her she wasn't doing enough was not her own voice, but a voice from the past, one that would not lead her toward her current goals. Once the clarity was in place to define her own personal goals, that voice faded into the background.

There are dramatic feisty moments, like my story, where the rule makers had to add new rules to the policy book such as "no birth deliveries on campus." Then there are more subtle feisty moments, like choosing self-care over productivity, and fun and play over doing dishes.

I see you, still here for my story. That tells me that you are with me. That you are brave and out-of-the-box. It tells me that your story, my friend, has its own flavor of feisty.

Let me ask you: How does your flavor of feisty show up in your relationships? Is it all smooth sailing, or like many, are there parts of that feistiness that are hard to navigate on your own?

There are a multitude of us ready to embrace your journey. My clients are all like you in their feisty independence. I walk alongside them as an ally, to help navigate the interpersonal relationships that are shifting, as they become a more radical version of themselves.

Let's rewrite your rulebook. Together.

About the Author

Stephanie Galindo is an interpersonal communication and relationship Coach for fellow neurodivergents/ADHDers. She helps them differentiate the voices of society from their own voice and take control over the areas of relationships, boundaries, and time management, through the lens of her 4 signature pillars: Self-Acceptance, Clarity, Accountability, and Self Coaching. Her unique program is 6 months of unlimited coaching to turn mountains into molehills and teach the client to begin self-coaching independently as new challenges arise.

Although she is from the US, she spent formative years in Tbilisi, Republic of Georgia, and has traveled internationally since childhood. She is currently adventuring in her RV with her husband, two boys, and a labradoodle.

https://linktr.ee/stephaniegalindocoaching

FINDERS, KEEPERS

BY LESLIE COLLINS BARBER

Casey woke to the blaring of the alarm. Her heart raced, shooting adrenalin through her body, as she normally woke up at least an hour before her set time. That hour of peace and quiet before she had to kick into high gear was the only time all day when she felt calm. Now she would have to hit the ground running, hoping that somehow the day would flex and provide her with a little respite one way or another.

Today was not to be that day, unfortunately.

She threw off the covers, slipping her feet into her well-worn slippers, being careful not to disturb Rick. She hurried downstairs, simultaneously turning on the coffee pot, throwing three English muffins into the toaster oven, letting the dogs out, unloading the dishwasher, and putting laundry in the dryer. Then she dashed upstairs to wake up Emily, Declan and Lily. She went through this ritual every morning, threatening the kids with bodily harm if they did not get up and get dressed for the bus.

As the coffee steamed suggestively in her mug, Casey bagged up chips and cookies and made sandwiches for their lunches, slathered the English muffins in butter and honey or jam or avocado, depending on which of her three children were eating what this week.

Lily had read that avocado toast was all the rage, so all she wanted was avocado everything. Emily had a sweet tooth and preferred honey. And Declan, sweet Declan, just wanted "butter, please."

As the kids finally started appearing, in varying states of appearance, Casey picked her battles. *Deodorant for everyone! Please brush your teeth!* Messy hair was a choice and matching clothes and socks was a battle she had long given up on. Why had she agreed to three kids in four years? Now three teenagers, they loved her desperately and gave her hell on a constant basis. Rick got off easy. She had to do the heavy lifting with household and family management, always having to be the hard ass, which was exhausting.

As the kids left for school, she glanced at her calendar, noting that she had a busy day ahead: doctor appointment for her mom, PTA meeting and a board meeting.

"Casey!!!!" Rick's yelling broke the silence. *What now?* "Why didn't you wake me up? I have a meeting this morning!"

"I am not your mother. You know that!" She yelled back.

Once she realized she would be the last to get to shower, she picked up the phone, "Hi mom, please make sure you are dressed and ready to go. I'll be there to pick you up in about an hour. I am running a little bit late, but you know I am always on time to your appointments."

Carolyn Wright relied heavily on Casey for her well-being. A widow for 30 years, she had never felt comfortable making her own decisions, resisting outside support and expecting Casey to pick up the slack. Now Carolyn was battling breast cancer, meaning Casey had to up her game, which meant getting Carolyn to the clinic weekly for her chemotherapy as well as a myriad of other appointments. Just making it through the summer was a miracle, as Carolyn was afraid to be alone after surgery. Casey had spent most of the summer at Carolyn's house, waiting on her. She never let Carolyn know that it was hard on her, feeling that if she was a good caregiver, then her own kids would be good to her when she was old, too.

Rick stomped through the kitchen, griping at Casey. He poured coffee into a to-go mug, threw open the refrigerator, grumbling about a lack of food. "I hate running late. This is an important meeting. I wish you would have remembered that. Today is going to be really stressful." He didn't make eye contact with Casey as he said this, walking out the door, and slamming it extra hard.

Tears came to Casey's eyes. All she did was give everything to everyone. She felt like a cliché. Magazine articles and chick lit were written about women like her. How did she end up like this? Where was the joy in her life? Her support network had dwindled and she was feeling sad that she didn't have anyone to talk to about her feelings.

She looked at the clock and realized that she had to be at her mom's in 45 minutes and still hadn't showered. Shit.

Fast-forward to later that week: Casey is paying bills online when the doorbell rings. Casey jumps up as the dogs go ballistic, rushing to murder the intruder. A FedEx driver is at the door, holding a large envelope.

"Casey Rogers? I have documents that require a signature."

Casey signs for the envelope and shuts the door. It is addressed to her, sent from a legal firm in Wyoming. She doesn't know anyone in Wyoming, but remembers that her dad's family lived there once, long ago, before she was born. He died when she was a teenager, and she has drifted apart from that side of the family.

Sitting down at the table, she carefully opens the envelope. Inside, she finds a ream of legal documents with her name on them. She shakes the envelope and a set of keys falls out. After a quick skim, she comes to realize that her grandfather has apparently left her some property. Strangely, it is property in the neighboring town, not in Wyoming. She rereads the paperwork a couple more times before grabbing her car keys and rushing out the door.

7203 W Lakeshore Drive. The address is burned into her brain. Why hadn't anyone ever told her about this home? Casey is confused and excited as she parks along the road. At the bottom of a steep, curving driveway is a small cabin facing the lake. There are leaves and debris piled around, indicating that it has been vacant for some time. Stands of evergreens shield the cabin from other homes.

Dark green paint is peeling off the siding, the yellow trim in need of a fresh coat. The front door is a cheerful red and there is a deck that wraps all the way around, seemingly well-built. Casey tries to peer in the windows, trying not to scare anyone if there happens to be someone inside.

Her heart is pounding. Nobody knows where she is. Towering cedar trees surround the home, shading it and hiding it from neighboring homes. Nobody would know the cabin was here unless they came looking for it. She knocks on the door and waits.

Casey's hands are shaking as she puts the key in the lock and opens the door, not knowing at all what to expect. The hinges squeak as the door swings open. Casey blinks a few times as her eyes adjust to the dim light. Heavy curtains are drawn over most of the windows, and the electricity is off, so it's hard to see. As she opens the curtains, the light reflecting off the lake fills the little cabin. It is small, but quaint, with pine floor and walls. *People on Pinterest would have a heyday with the bones of this place*, she thinks. There is a small kitchen, a tiny bathroom, and through an arched doorway, a little bedroom with a big built-in loft bed.

"*This is a love nest!*" she thinks. "*My grandpa had a love nest!*" She sits down cross-legged in the center of the empty room, her mind racing.

Casey calls the attorney in Wyoming, trying to find out the story behind this cabin and how she came to possess the keys. She wants to scream, CAN I KEEP THIS A SECRET?

Apparently, when Casey's dad died, her grandfather had put the cabin into her name and filed it with his attorney. Nobody had realized it was there until recently, discovered through an office purge. Now, the title is in Casey's name and it is all hers. HERS! Her dream of having a secret getaway has come true.

Home again, Casey hid in her bedroom, searching for ideas on how to have a secret cabin. There was very little information out there, so she decided just to wing it for now and hope for the best.

Rick came home late from work in a horrible mood after a particularly rough day at work, which would usually result in arguments and door slamming. Tonight, however, Casey wasn't willing to engage in his antics and just ignored his bullshit. He got frustrated because she wasn't listening to his woes, but seeing there was nothing he could do about it, he went and watched TV with a beer while she sat at the kitchen counter, leafing through a home improvement magazine, inspired like never before.

Casey looked at her calendar for the next day and quickly and swiftly cancelled her hair appointment, her lunch with Lori, her planning meeting with the drama department, and rescheduled a dentist appointment. Thankfully none of those things were life-threatening, and Carolyn's chemo wasn't until next week. With a clear day ahead, she made a to-do list of what she needed to make the cabin her own. After all the years of neglect, it would take some elbow grease and some simple furnishings to make the cabin a wonderful little retreat. It was still hard for her to wrap her head around the fact that it was hers and that nobody knew about it!

The next morning, she woke two hours before her alarm, making sure she dressed and showered well in advance of having to wake up the family. Rick was confused when Casey woke him up on time with a cup of coffee and a kiss. She sent him off to work with a hug and a smile, something different for both of them, as lately it had been nothing but angst and anger. Casey was desperate for everyone to leave, and time was dragging. As she heard Rick's car pulling away from the house, she pulled on her coat, grabbed her list, and ran out of the house to get on with the debut of her secret life.

She checked off the items on her list quickly, finding it surprisingly easy to get things established in her own name. A PO Box, a bank account, plus some gardening and cleaning supplies, and she was on her way to *her cabin*. She fought back tears of joy as she began scrubbing the bathroom. *Her bathroom.* Soon it was time to go home and be a mom again, so she put the supplies away. Never had she been so sad to stop cleaning. The pure joy she had felt all day long was unlike anything she had experienced. Her life was opening up in a way that she had never expected. A place of her own, a secret place... all hers.

Is this a dream? How is this happening to me??

The weekend arrived, leaving Casey stuck at home with the family, unable to escape to the cabin, yet unable to think of anything else. Her mind constantly dwelled on her own little space, where she decorated and redecorated her perfect getaway. Her family looked at her oddly, as she was no longer herself. Instead, she was distracted and had a constant half-smile on her face, her eyes fixed somewhere in the distance as she focused on her secret, her new future that had been dropped into her lap. Lacrosse, soccer, a school play… she attended all with ease, chatting briefly with the other moms, yet not fully engaged in their discourse, leaving them wondering what was going on with her. They knew her mom was in cancer treatment, so they just assumed she was busy with that, and let her go on her way without too much thought. Little did they know that Casey's secret was something each and every one of them had fantasized about for years.

Rick had noticed Casey's distant stare, finally asking her about it on Sunday evening. "What is going on with you this weekend? It's like you are a million miles away from here. Are you OK? Is it your mom?"

"Yes, yeah, um, my mom's been on my mind a lot. She has a lot of needs right now, and I'm trying to figure out how to spend more time with her in the next few months. The holidays are coming and that's when she gets really stressed out. I don't want you all to think I am neglecting you, but I will be with her quite a bit as she finishes up chemo and starts getting back into her own daily life." *It's a great excuse to be gone a lot! Mom never talks to Rick, he'll never know.*

"Of course, hun, I know she needs you. Don't worry about anything, we'll make do here, even if we have to keep on ordering pizza for every meal." He was only half-joking, as every time she was gone, he tended to order pizza, even if she was just out with a friend for the evening. His lack of cooking skills was remarkable.

On Monday, Casey had to take Carolyn to chemotherapy, so she couldn't get over to the cabin for the day. She needed to buy some furniture, just a few things, to make the cabin habitable once she finished cleaning. After she dropped her mom at home, she hit Crawford's Furniture and found a few things for the cabin. A comfy couch for reading and napping, a cozy chair, a couple of tables with lamps, a mattress—just the basics. With her new bank account, she was able to finance the purchase, arranging for a quick delivery. *This is so easy! I don't know why or how, but everything is just falling right into place!*

The rest of her week was busy as usual, with meetings, sports and appointments, but she was adept at finding the small windows of time to dash over to the cabin and polish it up in preparation for the furniture's arrival the following week. By Friday evening, it was spotless and ready. She had removed most of the heavy curtains and the natural light that shone in made the cabin look stunning in the evening light. Once she had her furniture and lighting, it would be just perfect. *One more weekend to get through, one more chemo for mom, and my new life starts.*

Finally, it was Tuesday again. Casey had cleared her schedule in order to be ready to receive the furniture and set up the cabin. Rick had been suffering a cold all weekend, and she was worried that he was going to stay home and attempt to derail her plans. Luckily, he had a meeting, so he begrudgingly left, with sloping shoulders and shuffling feet dragging out to the car as he tried to get pity from Casey. She didn't even notice; she was too excited. In the trunk of her car were bags of goodies she'd bought over the weekend for the cabin —a small set of dishes, some sheets, pillows and towels, candles and a couple of framed pictures and some artwork to have around the place to make it seem more homey. That's all she needed right now.

She arrived at the cabin just ahead of the delivery truck. They were early! She peered around at her neighbors' driveways but didn't see anyone around since most everyone had left for the season. As they carried her furniture in, she urged them mentally *hurry, hurry, hurry! I don't want anyone to see!*

Once she was alone, she sat on the new couch, and then laid down, her head sinking into the soft pillow. She got up and sat in the chair, turning on the lamp, crossing and uncrossing her legs, leaning left and right, discovering all the ways in which she could be comfortable in her new space.

Casey looked around and thought *what the hell*. She took off all her clothes and laid naked on the mattress. She walked into the bathroom, into the kitchen, even opened the door and stepped out on the deck, carefully peering around to see if anyone could see her. She already knew that the deck was very secluded. Being naked was scary to her, her vulnerability pushing up against her newfound independence.

She walked back through the cabin, looking at herself in the bathroom mirror. Her middle-aged body was still firm, with some softening around the edges. Her eyes were full of fire. Something was alive and burning in her now, a new unstoppable force. She reached out and touched the mirror, running her hands down the lines of her face. She didn't recognize the person she was now, a different woman than the one who had driven away from her family this morning. She didn't know what to do next. Whatever she did, it would be great, it would be exciting, and it would be all hers.

About the Author

Up-and-coming author Leslie Collins Barber hails from the beautiful Pacific Northwest. It is her goal to help women find their power and manifest their best lives. Blurring the line between fiction and nonfiction, Leslie draws from her own diverse life experiences to explore women's unmet needs and desires that are rooted in great potential. Her upcoming fiction series, *Gap Year*, unleashes a movement that will inspire others to gain confidence and find the motivation to achieve their biggest dreams.

https://linktr.ee/lesliebarber

WE THREE FEISTY WOMEN

I AM MY MOTHERS' DAUGHTER

BY SAGE TAYLOR KINGSLEY

T his is a tale of not one feisty woman, but three.

Our story begins in the summer of 1964: "The Summer of Love."

A 20-year-old college student in Ohio enjoyed her first passionate encounter.

Some months later, she had an important decision to make.

Her boyfriend offered to marry her. But something inside her protested: "He's not the one I should settle down with."

Her mother and others pressured her to abort the baby. But a fierce voice within told her, "No. I'm going to have this baby. I'll find a good home for my child. And someday, I'll find her again."

So you see, my very being in this world was a result of my birth mother's strength of character. It guided her to neither take the conventional, expected route (marriage) nor the shamed, make-this-problem-disappear route (abortion).

Meanwhile, a 34-year-old woman in New York was making another feisty choice.

She wanted another baby, a sibling for her 7-year-old daughter, but due to fertility issues, she was unable to get pregnant. So she coerced, coaxed and cajoled her husband until he agreed: "OK! Let's adopt."

And sure enough, by these women's empowered choices, I was raised in New York by my adoptive parents, with one big sister.

And their choices around motherhood were not the only ways in which both of my mothers have been feisty.

Joyce, my birth mother whom I affectionately call my "firstmother," dedicated her life to helping disadvantaged mothers, children, and the disabled, and even founded a charity, Bali Children's Project.

When traveling in Bali, she was dismayed to learn that most families would send only one child, typically the eldest boy, to school.

Tens of thousands of girls were missing any opportunity to do anything more than harvest rice, be a house servant, or a temple dancer at best.

Joyce and her husband, John, devoted many years and dollars to send girls to school. They built schools and libraries, trained teachers, and provided essentials like uniforms, school supplies, even family members' surgeries.

When you speak with her, you'd never suspect that this soft-spoken soul is not only a globe trotter but a world changer who brought hope to hundreds through education and compassionate action.

When I turned 16, she began her long-planned search: to find news of me and, with hope of a miracle, to reunite with me.

She began with the usual methods. She called the hospital.

A nurse insisted, "Ma'am, you never gave birth to a child in this hospital."

Joyce got feisty: "Don't you tell ME I didn't have a baby there! I most certainly did."

She attended meeting after meeting of birthparents. She made friends, many of whom found their children, in ways both heartening and heartbreaking.

Years passed. Still, she could not find me.

Until one day, another birth mother told her of a secret detective known only as St. Jude, named for the patron saint of lost causes.

Arrangements were made, information was whispered, often in the middle of the night. Joyce never knew his real name, never met him, but he promised he would find her daughter.

More years passed. Everyone told Joyce to let it go. To accept her loss and move on with her life.

But she never gave up hope.

One night, around 4 a.m., the phone rang.

St. Jude asked, "Would you like to know what your daughter is doing this summer?"

Joyce ecstatically replied, "Yes!!!"

"She is helping disabled children with cerebral palsy, in Queens."

Joyce exclaimed, "That's my girl!"

Because her twin sister had Down Syndrome, one of Joyce's life-long causes has been to help people with developmental disabilities, so she took this as a Sign from the Universe that I was indeed her daughter.

We never did discover why it was so hard for Joyce to find me, nor how the mysterious St. Jude located me. We believe the adoption lawyer covered the records via a "gray market adoption." Only by her extreme devotion was she able to find me.

In many ways, I am a lot like my firstmother: both writers with missions to make the world a better place.

So for Joyce, here is my definition-poem of Feisty (let's call it a "Feistygram" for fun):

F Feminist
E Educating
I Intelligent
S Supportive
T Talented
Y Youth

My adoptive mom, Lillian, a Jewish New Yorker, is as different from "Berkeley hippie" Joyce as two women can be, yet they share an inner determination to not let others limit them.

Lillian traveled 3 hours daily to her position as a Manhattan legal secretary.

It took courage for her to initiate a divorce in 1976, due to a loveless and sexless marriage.

She came out of her divorce as a lively, passionate disco dancer, and let's just say she made up for lost time when it came to getting her sensual needs met. Go, Mom!

My mom has always been my biggest supporter. I was raised with the beliefs: "You can do anything you set your mind to do," and "To thine own self be true."

In 2008, a tremendous opportunity appeared for me, which got my business on the map: I was invited to present on self-love (which I was writing a book about) to 930 people at T. Harv Eker's "All Your Relations" conference, sharing the stage with Marianne Williamson.

My challenges were:
* I'd never spoken on a big stage before.
* I'd never used Powerpoint.
* I didn't even own a laptop.

I asked God: "Can I do this??!"

And the answer I got was: "This is your Golden Portal you've been manifesting! Go for it! Your angels will be with you all the way. Why do you think we call it 'winging it'?"

I had eight days to finish my book, get a laptop, learn PowerPoint, write my presentation, fly to San Diego and DO IT. My mom loaned me $2,000 so I could buy a laptop. I paid her back immediately after selling $9,000 of self-love books in 90 love-drenched minutes.

This experience changed me so much because since then, I've always known that I AM A WOMAN WHO can bring nearly 1,000 people to healing tears and smiles, hearts glowing, even though I'd had little speaking experience to speak of. Gutsy!

My mom can be bossy, yet she's also generous, puts family first, walks her talk, and is a great example of a woman who knows what she wants and won't stop until she gets it!

She learned how to drive at the ripe young age of 65. Mom has macular degeneration and no longer drives, but she still dances, expresses herself like a boss to everyone within earshot, and acts "not a day over 39." NO ONE believes she is 90.

For Lillian, Feisty stands for:

F Family

E Encouraging

I Inspiring

S Strong

T Tough

Y Young at Heart

And me? I am a living, breathing, shining example of Nature Feist + Nurture Feist.

I feel I've got the best of both my bold mamas. My kids agree that I'm a feisty mama in my own right.

I've had opportunities to "find my feist" in many life areas including health, wealth, visibility, home, love, and family.

I was born with an immunodeficiency disorder, Natural Killer Cell Disease. My NK cells, crucial white blood cells in the body's first line of defense are.... pacifists. Yup. They just don't do enough killing.

This wasn't diagnosed until my 40s. I felt strangely relieved to learn that there was a medical REASON why I'd been so sick. I was not a hypochondriac. Now I understood *why* my immune system was weak, *why* I almost died 20+ times from respiratory infections.

I've worked with more health-care practitioners utilizing more modalities than I can count, from acupuncturists and chiropractors to immunologists and naturopaths. I got trained and certified in hypnotherapy and Reiki and have woven an ever-changing life-support web around me and within me.

In 1994, I experienced an unexpected, profound spiritual initiation, complete with three Near Death Experiences in 18 hours, in the Mexican desert. Each NDE featured a life-saving miracle that also expanded my Third Eye exponentially.

I began to see auras, channel Angels, do intuitive readings and healings. I wrote a book on self-love, and taught workshops about enlightenment and personal growth. I wrote hundreds of songs and poems with such ease, it was like taking dictation.

Yet even after being accelerated to a level of creativity, inner peace, and divine bliss that most people don't even know is possible, I still struggled with finances, health, frequent moves, and unhealed pain around both of my mothers.

My husband and I lost our home in 2006 in the Equity Bubble Burst. We started over, moved to Hawaii, where we were homeless for awhile, staying in hotels and couch surfing, with a 3- and 7-year-old.

I dusted off my teaching credential and taught middle school English.

My teaching career came to a sudden halt when a student whom I had caught cheating on a test threatened to kill me. I collapsed and became agoraphobic. I hid in bed for months, afraid of... everything.

One day, my 5-year-old climbed into bed with me and stroked my cheek.

He said softly, "Mommy? When are you coming back?"

I burst into tears.

I realized that I had a choice.

And I chose life.

I came back. Back into my body, back into our world. For my children.

Soon after my son brought me back with his love, I had a conversation with God that went something like this:

"Hello, God? It's me. I know I'm here to teach people about love and spirit. I'm willing to do anything You put me here to do. BUT I am NOT willing to keep suffering anymore! I am DONE with these health and wealth challenges. It's ridiculous. Please, show me the way!"

And the message I received was: "Sage. You already have all the tools you need. Use the tools you teach to others. Redesign your relationship with money and with your body, from the inside out."

Aha!

I created a powerful meditation audio integrating 14 healing modalities including hypnosis, visualization, dreamwork, prayer, breathwork, and chakra healing. Within 90 days of listening to *Aligning with Abundance*, my right livelihood income skyrocketed from $200 to $4,000 a month. And I said goodbye to day jobs forever.

With help from above and those who love me, and using my tools in an innovative way, I empowered myself, and thousands of others, to create an entirely new prosperous life.

I decided to stop manifesting Near Death Experiences (NDEs) and to cherish **Fully Alive Experiences (FAEs)** instead.

My business as The Prosperous Goddess^R to date has generated over $1.6 million. For 12 years, I supported my family of four by doing what I loved: teaching retreats, online courses and workshops, and providing healing and coaching sessions, divinely designed to help women accelerate their empowerment, enlightenment and enrichment, in every sense.

One of my courses was voted the #1 Law of Attraction program worldwide by people in 18 countries. This was a great honor, but the best part was being able to help more people because of this recognition.

We often teach what we ourselves need to remember.

On my 50th birthday, my heart was wrenched apart when my birth mother did not show up for an intimate lunch intended to celebrate my first 50 years and bless me for the next 50.

Instead of feeling honored, I spent an hour wailing so hard, it was as if someone had died. I felt like this was proof that she never loved me, that I was never good enough, that I would never be lovable...

All my inner child abandonment traumas were triggered. I felt devastated.

She later apologized. But the primal adoption wound, my baby-self not being seen, my baby-self not being breastfed or heard or held or loved, all smacked me so hard, I went into a deep depression.

I had low contact with Joyce for two years.

In that time, I dove deep.

And I healed my mother wounds.

I also healed other childhood and ancestral patterns (just because my mothers are feisty doesn't mean they're perfect).

I healed MANY ways in which I felt like I never REALLY belonged in *either* family.

I learned how to connect with the Divine Mother, how to awaken my feminine essence, and clear my entire ancestral lineage, both nature and nurture, because my mothers' ways of "failing me" in how they mothered me were the result of *their own issues with their mothers*, and on down the line. I discovered Nine Sacred Gates to Healing the Mother Wound.

I began supporting clients with mother wound healing, unraveling levels, layers and lifetimes of traumas that they had been bearing, often unconsciously and energetically (you can take a free quiz and learn more at: www.MotherWoundHealing.com/quiz).

When we heal our mother wounds, we heal our relationship to the Sacred Feminine, with the Earth and our bodies, and we reclaim our innate right to THRIVE and be fully ALIVE.

We liberate our very souls.

And we reclaim our power – and our ability to love ourselves and life itself.

If you've been around the block a few times like me, you've learned by now that the one thing we can count on in life is change, right?

Fast forward to February 2020. The world changed for all of us with Covid-19, and my husband made a disclosure to me that was the nail in the coffin for our marriage of 23 years.

Not only did I get slammed by the Life Reset Button by sheltering in place and seven family members getting Covid, including my husband, but I saw my business spiral downward rapidly.

Miraculously, I did not get very sick. Proof that my immune system healing protocols were working, that my deep mother wound healing also boosted my immune system, and a sign that God really only DOES give us as much as we can handle (thank you!).

I had to / got to navigate my way through the divorce, in a way that was loving, consciously uncoupling while staying good friends. My Life Reset also included selling our home, buying a home of my own for the first time, relocating, moving myself, my two sons, my furbabies, and my mom into it -- then moving my mom OUT.

We could NOT get along living together, and thanks to my mother wound healing, my newly empowered Boundary Badass would not tolerate both of us being miserable. I found her a nice assisted living place nearby, and we get along wonderfully now.

Did the decline of my Prosperous Goddess biz happen because of Covid and people no longer valuing personal growth as a high priority at a time of chaos? Sure.

Or did my business wind down because I was going within to heal mother wound trauma and divorce grief, preparing to birth something, and someone, new? AbSOULutely!

I needed a year to heal, and to gently let go of that version of me.

I am so full of gratitude and grace that today I enjoy a deeply loving relationship with BOTH of my feisty mothers (and they even love each other!).

We are always evolving, on a spiral path of life.

I took the time I needed to recover my energy, and to rediscover who I am today, and who I desire to be tomorrow.

Every breakdown can also be a breakthrough.

And what I Real-Eyesed (saw with my inner vision) was that the ONE thing I have always loved to do most was WRITING.

I wrote my first book, poem, and song, all at age nine.

For me, writing is as easy as breathing.

I also love to edit. I am that Eagle-Eyed Ms. Meticulous who improves and elevates EVERY piece of writing (in a kind way). My backgrounds in journalism, teaching English, and as a best-selling author, poet and proofreader all came to the forefront.

Drumroll, please!

I launched my NEWEST business baby: **Sage for Your Page,** providing intuitive copywriting and book editing.

I'd been editing books since 1991 and writing copy for my clients who discovered that they needed a website, emails or book to share their message, after I helped them step confidently into their purpose.

Pivoting at age 56 took a lot of TRUST: in myself, in others, and in my Universe (YOUniverse or Yoniverse).

I am now happily in my next phase, writing my own chapter, not only in *Feisty*, but in my life.

I continue to touch lives through transformational Prosperous Goddess online courses (including Mother Wound Healing), and I'm delighted that my natural Superpower playing with words is helping more women, visionaries, healers, coaches, spiritual entrepreneurs, authors and paradigm shifters to shine more brightly, to live more joyfully, and to thrive more abundantly.

Words create worlds.

I love myself for honoring my callings in life, and for calling this forth in others.

Because we were all put here to do GREAT things with GREAT love.

And for me? My Feistygram is:

F Free
E Energy
I Intuitive
S Spiritual
T Thinker
Y Yes!!!

THANK you for allowing me to share "We Three Feisty Women" with you.

Now it's your turn. I invite you to take time right now to reflect about your own journey.

What's YOUR Feistygram?

I'm cheering you on! I'd love to hear from you.

.   .   .

"YOUR FEISTINESS IS YOUR FABULOUSNESS.
  Your fierceness is your freedom.
  Your fire is your fulfillment.
  Don't dim your light – shine brighter.
  Don't squelch your desires – speak out!
  The world needs you, and YOU need you,
  to be ALL of who you are,
  and the time is now
  and yesterday
  and tomorrow
  and always."
  - Sage Taylor Kingsley

About the Author

SAGE Taylor Kingsley is a wordsmith who thinks like a marketer, intuits like an oracle, and moves energy like a shaman. A Caring and Careful Book Copy Editor, Perfectionistic Proofreader, and Wow-Inducing Wordsmith, Sage honors your voice and vision while enhancing and elevating eloquently.

The Prosperous Goddess^R and Sage for Your Page^{TM} have magne-tized over $1.6 million from copy. As a coach and copywriter, Sage helps healers, coaches & creatives heartfully invite, ignite and incite sales and expand their reach through aligned words of power that change the world.

SAGE is also a compassionate Mother Wound Healer helping daughters (and sons) of narcissistic or emotionally absent mothers, adoptees and others become fully liberated from their ancestral lineage and inner child trauma, across ALL generations. SAGE is a mystic poet, #1 best-selling author, hypnotherapist, mom, Reiki Master -- and lover of life.

Words are her playground, her magic wand, and her canvas. Voted the world's #1 Law of Attraction teacher, SAGE passionately empowers you to connect with the Divine, Prosper, Thrive & SHINE!

Connect with Sage and receive FREE GIFTS including *The Mother Wound Quiz, 10 Keys to Kick-Ass Copy That Converts* and more at:

http://linktr.ee/sagetheprosperousgoddess

FEISTY = LIFE

BY SUREKHA RAGHAVAN

What does it mean to be Feisty?

For me, growing up in a traditional migrant Indian family in Malaysia, it was recognizing very early in my childhood that there were clearly delineated rules and roles of behavior -- and that even the smallest step outside those roles and rules was considered to be *feisty* and therefore *unacceptable*.

Looking back from my 50s though, I think of "being feisty" as being "normal" and even as being critical to being *alive*.

It is not a calling to simply "break rules."

It is a calling to LIVE.

Looking back now, I know that I never intended to be "feisty," as in I never consciously decided to do things a little "differently" or cause conflict. And looking back now, I realize that feistiness for me was how my actions were *perceived* rather than *intended*. For me, those actions weren't chosen to be difficult.

Those choices for me were not *choices*. For me, I had *no* choice.

Let me explain.

I grew up in a loving family, the youngest of three, and my parents were always looking out for my best interests. They were migrants from India, coming to Malaysia to make some money and intending to go back and settle in India.

When it was time for me to go to school, they chose to put me in a British International school, where the medium of instruction was in English (the local schools were being taught in Bahasa Malaysia, the native language of Malaysia). The intention was that we could eventually all go back to India and I could continue in school there. But it was a move they kept postponing, and ultimately never made.

In hindsight, this decision exposed me to a world that was very different from the cultural norms of my parents, who were traditional and conservative. My school had 42 different nationalities and suddenly I was exposed to all sorts of different cultures, languages, ways of living. And I LOVED it. There was an openness and an acceptance of differences and mutual respect. And just as suddenly, it became clear to me that this "other" world was not seen as being part of my parents' world. As they would put it, "Their way is not our way." And I realized at a very young age that I really did prefer "their way." Oh dear.

And so we come to one night when my parents and I were out somewhere in our family car when I was 6 or 7 years old and they were trying to impress on me the importance of speaking my mother tongue, Malayalam. I had been fluent in it right up to the time when I went to school. My parents were fluent in English too and both languages were used freely at home, but it was clear that I was using more English than Malayalam at home.

My parents had an arranged marriage. All of the "Aunties" and "Uncles" that we knew in our Indian community had arranged marriages too, and we frequently attended those weddings as well. For some reason, it was something I did not want to have, even at the age of 6! I just knew that it was *not* for me. And sitting at the back of the car that night, my 6 year old brain thought, "Well, if I don't speak Malayalam, I won't be able to have an arranged marriage!" And *that* was my first conscious, outwardly perceived "feisty" decision. I couldn't consciously explain this to my parents. I just knew that they wouldn't understand.

All I did that night, at the back of the car, was stay silent to their requests to speak my mother tongue. To their credit, they never punished me for that, and we continued with them speaking to me in English or Malayalam and I only ever responded in English. I do understand my mother tongue today and I can speak it a tiny bit, but my tongue can't quite get around those words any more. It was only many, many years later that I recognized this as my first realization that I was clearly in the category of being *different.*

Being *different* has its challenges in any society, but in Asian society, it can be incredibly emotionally difficult too. If one strayed from the accepted ways of behavior, punishment was swift and second chances were few. I witnessed families being torn apart by children choosing to marry others outside their community. Parents would not speak to them again for many years and those relationships were always awkward and strained. We always had to stay within the fold and never stray. Any movement outside, however small, was seen as being "feisty."

I tried my best to not stray. I followed the rules as much as possible. Fortunately, because I loved my school, I studied hard and brought home good results. I was a quiet, well-behaved child and student, viewed as shy and quiet by most other people within my community. But the "quietness" was more because I knew I had more radical and even *revolutionary* thoughts in my head that I knew wouldn't be accepted. I "flew under the radar" as it were, for as long as possible.

So what were the accepted "ways of behavior" for an Indian girl/woman in my culture?

To study hard, go to university, get married, and have children. This was the way to "live happily ever after." Because I was the youngest, and a girl, I think my parents made concessions for me. When it came time to go to university, I chose to do Social Work and my parents accepted that. But I found university in Singapore very disillusioning after my very liberal early education and I dropped out in the middle of the second year, with my parents' support but also their dismay. They supported my decision to try again by going to university in England. But whereas I wanted to study my favorite subject, English Literature, my father wanted me to do something more "sensible" like Law. I acquiesced by applying to do either Law or English and they allowed me to choose, depending on what I was accepted for. I have to say that my parents did try very hard to support me in my choices. I could see that they only wanted the best for me. But for me, after the nightmare of dropping out of one university, all I wanted was to enjoy what I was doing in another.

This was the problem. Personal happiness was not seen to be a sensible pursuit. English Literature was not seen as a sensible option. It was only when I said I could go into teaching that my parents supported this choice. It became increasingly clear to me that following my heart and my joy was seen as a challenge to the status quo. It was seen as going against the grain and upsetting the apple cart.

I saw it as following my heart and joy. They saw it as being FEISTY.

My years in England were some of my happiest. There was one other Malaysian student in the English department when I arrived, who was there on a scholarship. When she left, there was just me. ONE Malaysian student in the entire English department! Which didn't bother me. After learning English Geography, History, and Literature all through my school years, it felt like coming home to be in England, and I got on really well with my classmates. The other Malaysians there regarded me as an oddity, not surprisingly, but that was all right. I knew now I was always going to be perceived as being different. And in England, away from the strictures of Asian rules, I was free to be me. Not a revolutionary, just someone following her heart.

I can see now that I was seen to be "feisty" when I chose to go against what was *expected* of me. When I chose to go against *societal* expectations. And when those expectations were seen as "rules," we were really in trouble. Rules are there for general order and safety. There are driving rules, for example, so that we can be safe when we drive on the road. I would not *ever* choose to drive on the wrong side of the road. But when I chose to do something for my own happiness, it was sometimes *seen* as driving on the wrong side of the road, doing the unconventional and unacceptable thing.

To my parents' relief, I fell in love with a man from our community and we got married with their blessings. But unfortunately, it seemed inevitable that we would clash, just as I had with my own culture. He told me once that I was a coconut, brown outside and white inside, and that really does sum up why we clashed. Again, I was clashing against another world of rules and expectations.

There are many reasons why the marriage failed and there was definitely fault on both sides. The deciding factor for me was when I suggested the separation to my husband, he said to me that we should stay together "out of duty" rather than love. That that was what our parents would do. Again, I was faced with the choice of following Indian/Asian society's expectations and unwritten rules. He was willing to stay together and be miserable. I was not. I wanted a chance at happiness. For *all* of us, for him, for me and for our two sons, who were only 4 and 11 at the time.

I chose the feisty option. I left the marriage. Being "feisty" here was not about being difficult or intentionally going against the grain. It was about choosing LIFE and happiness. For me, there was no choice. I *had* to leave the marriage.

My life since then has not been easy. I had been diagnosed with bipolar disorder at the tail end of the marriage and I struggled with that as did both my sons. But—and this is key—I am living my life on my own terms. And my sons have become kind and compassionate people through our experiences together.

An older lady from my community said to me recently that my life was a mess. From her perspective, I hadn't followed the standard "prescription" for how my life should go: go to university, get married, have children and live happily ever after. But that was her perception. From my perspective, it seemed to me that the universe was always testing me. Was I going to give in and follow the beaten path and be miserable? Or was I going to make a leap of faith and take the "feisty" untrodden path?

My life wasn't a mess. It was just different.

Life is far more rewarding and enriching when we take the brave and untrodden path. It is not always easy to follow our hearts and follow our bliss. There will be family and friends and co-workers saying, "Don't be silly, that won't work" and they will try and persuade you to stay "on course." From choosing to do Literature, I did end up teaching it in my old school for a while, which I enjoyed immensely. But life and marriage brought me to Australia and my own spiritual healing journey here has led me to do Tarot readings now and spiritual healing work.

Doing the readings and the healing gives me a great deal of JOY and I have helped a lot of people. As Thoreau put it, "The mass of men lead lives of quiet desperation." If I had chosen to follow my culture's expectations, I have no doubt that I would be living that life too.

Choose to be Feisty. Choose LIFE. Do what makes your heart sing. What others perceive to be feisty is just joy calling you to dance in its path.

It continues to amaze me everyday, how even little things are considered to be "revolutionary." At the markets one day, I happened upon one half of a pretty pair of earrings. The stall owner gave it to me for free and when I went home, I wore them with another earring that didn't match, of course. But it gives me JOY to wear this earring in this way. And now, I deliberately do this all the time. I wear mismatched earrings all the time just for the fun of it. The sky hasn't fallen in and I haven't hurt anyone by breaking this unwritten rule that earrings have to match. A friend said to me about them once, "I can't do what you do and wear earrings like that." Even such a small break in convention made her feel uncomfortable.

Isn't it interesting how we follow so many "rules" so unconsciously and how uncomfortable and guilty we feel when we choose not to follow them? I invite you to look at your life too and see if maybe you are doing the same thing.

I am not suggesting, by any means, that we make grand sweeping changes just for the heck of it. But why not be a bit different, just for the FUN of it?! My Christmas tree is up all year too. That, too, seems to be a cardinal rule that can't be broken. But it is so pretty when I put the lights on too and brings a smile to my face when I see it. We are not talking about rules for safety here, but arbitrary rules that were made by someone somewhere for some purpose then. Am I *really* causing a problem by wearing mismatched earrings and keeping my Christmas tree up? If that is considered to be feisty, so be it!

Choose life, and choose to follow your heart. While I can't guarantee that the journey will be easy, I can quite certainly say that the journey will bring you more joy and less predictability and quiet desperation. When I decided to choose life and happiness, it was perceived as being "difficult." The same may be true for you. Don't let that deter you.

It is your own life after all. How would you like to live it? Being Feisty, I hope!

About the Author

Surekha Raghavan is a Tarot Reader and Spiritual Healer who helps her clients find Hope and meaning in their life journey. Her interests include Feng Shui, relationships and Oneness in diversity. Her work is inspired by a deep desire to help the world work together through community, cooperation and collaboration.

https://linktr.ee/Surekha_Raghavan

HOW I FOUND MY FEISTY

BY KIMBERLY JESSUP MARTIN

I was raised in the inner city of Philadelphia, the youngest of seven girls and one younger brother. By the time I was about eleven yrs. old, my mom was the only parent in the home.

Even though my family didn't have a lot, it didn't feel like I was missing out on anything. We did the same things as kids from two-parent households with more money. For example, we played with friends, never went without food or clean clothes to wear. Although my mother struggled with alcohol abuse, she took care of her children the best she could. In fact, she kept such an immaculate home, people would say you could eat off her floors.

I have experienced a lot of tragedy, and made some unwise decisions in my life. My unwise decisions and traumas left me pregnant at fourteen years old, raped at twenty, addicted to cocaine for over fifteen years, and physically and mentally abused throughout.

As I grew, I began to look for love in all the wrong places, which led to promiscuous behavior, craving attention from men who sometimes treated me badly. And because I had rarely seen a relationship that was loving and mutually respectful, being treated badly was my normal. Most of the relationships around me had some form of abuse, some subtle and some very visible. We learn from what we see and what we are taught, right or wrong.

I now understand that when we walk this journey of life in our own wisdom, strength, desires, will, and choices, we create the environment in which we live.

I continued in abusive relationships for years. But the addiction, rape, physical and mental abuse could never compare to the pain I felt in the tragedy that would change everything.

On September 3, 2000, my life changed forever in the span of one hour. That was the day my son took his own life in my presence.

He was at that time my only child, twenty-four years old. The pain I felt is indescribable. I was angry, mad, and confused. I felt like my insides could just burst, and I let out a sharp, high pitched, piercing scream that somehow seemed to release an ounce of the pain I was feeling in that moment. My world as I knew it was shattered.

My only child was gone, and I had witnessed it.

I would no longer be anyone's mother. There would be no one to love me just for me, even if I messed up or fell short. My heart was breaking, and my life would never, ever be the same. No one could tell me that, with time, my heart would heal. But I knew life must go on.

Tears still flow. Holidays and family gatherings are sometimes hard for me, when I see the children that are around the same age as my son. Some memories make you smile, and some make you cry. Thankfully, my son did give me the most beautiful grandchildren, whom I love dearly.

While writing this chapter, someone asked me about my thought process along the way, my turning points, how each situation was a stepping stone to my power. And when did I find my faith, or was it always there?

Raising my son at fifteen: I didn't even know I possessed any power. And the thought process? I was in survival mode. I had a baby I needed to take care of, and that was my focus. I don't think I even took time to process my thoughts.

My addiction: I wasn't thinking at that time in my life. I was in an environment where I tried a lot of things, not thinking about consequences, just pleasing my fleshly desires. Eventually I got tired of letting this drug control me and keep me from being the best person I could be. I knew life had more to offer me, and I wanted it.

My faith: It has always been there, but for many years I was the hindrance to my own faith. My son's death left me feeling powerless and questioning God. I wondered how my creator could allow a person of growing faith who was active in the church, preaching sermons, studying the bible faithfully, and building a closer relationship with Him, to go through such a tremendous loss.

Years later, there came a life-changing revelation through a familiar scripture, which catapulted me into finding out who I really was and gave me courage, power, and determination. That scripture was: "I will praise thee; for I am fearfully and wonderfully made: marvelous are thy works and my soul knows very well (Psalms 139:14)."

Two words in this scripture translated in the Hebrew language stuck out to me: **Fearfully**, meaning: reverence, heartfelt interest, and with respect; **Wonderfully**, meaning: unique and set apart. How remarkable that he who created the universe took time out to create me with reverence and respect; that I am unique and set apart. This scripture, along with all the other confirming scriptures of who I was created to be, and what I was created to do, made me realize I was given power and dominion on the earth. I was created by an all-knowing, all-powerful GOD. He knew about all my tragedies, pain, disappointments, and if I would just surrender to him and trust his plan for my life, I would be an overcomer. I would be victorious. And today, that is exactly who I am: a victorious overcomer.

You can be too. Just follow the plan he has for you.

We are loved unconditionally, no matter what we have done, or where we have been. Everything that happens in our lives, we can learn from, gain strength from, and teach others. Growth, wisdom, and knowledge come from the things we experience. No one can experience them for us. Knowledge is power in any form. All things work together for your good.

Once I began to understand who I was created to be, I began to walk in boldness. My faith increased, I used my voice to encourage, uplift, and comfort those who were hurting, those who felt that life had beaten them down and couldn't see any relief, and had thought about giving up. These are the women I want my voice to reach and to help make a difference in their lives.

Realizing this helped me show up differently in the world. I received confidence, determination, and courage, not so much because of who I was, in my own strength, but because of GOD's strength that lives in me, and it felt as if I was 6 ft tall, though I only stood at 5 ft. 2". When I would teach the word of GOD, I got bolder, and now I would witness to others from a place of confidence, not fear.

Also, I began to share my stories and not allow judgement of others to muzzle me. Women do not have to lose themselves to toxic situations. The fact is, we can learn, be helped, comforted, and also know that there is a way out if we continue to share our truth and be vulnerable.

This is the fuel that motivates me to keep sharing my life's journey with women who have walked similar paths, so they will know that you can overcome and be made whole again. Follow the blueprint (the Bible), hold on to your faith, and know that all things are possible. Forgive, even if you think they don't deserve it. It will free you. Know your worth and your purpose: you belong to the king, and you have everything you need.

I ask myself, "Can I help others?" I know I can, and I WILL.

I started a young women's ministry group through my church, where I taught women between the ages of fourteen and seventeen who were growing up in similar environments as myself. I taught these young women the Bible, what it means to be determined, courageous and confident. I let them know their voices matter, that they are worthy of love, and what self-respect means. In other words, I taught them to find THEIR feisty.

I hoped that the group would be a safe place for those young women to share their stories, fears, hopes, challenges, and experiences. It was, and they did. I prayed that there would be remarkable changes in the way they saw themselves, and that they would show up in the world as strong, confident young women, full of hope. Knowing by faith the power of GOD that resides in them. Knowing that they have the ability to do and be whatever they want to do or be by believing in themselves. Knowing that everything they need to succeed is already inside of them. Knowing that when obstacles come, which they will, they can get to the other side, not by trying to climb over it, or find a way around it, but by going through it. I taught them to stay on track, stay focused, don't give up, be determined, don't ever lose faith, and to remember they were created with purpose, and with reverence.

Most of the young ladies completed high school and a few continued on to college, my daughter being one of them. She is now in her sophomore year of college. I even shared some of my stories with them to let them know that I'm not as perfect as they might think. I wanted them to understand that things happen in life. If you fall down, it's okay. The problem begins if you don't get back up, dust yourself off, and continue your journey to become the best you: a productive, effective, powerful, purpose-driven woman graced by GOD with the ability to complete every assignment given you to do on Earth with the help of GOD. All these things are in reach.

For example, in 2017, I adopted a 7 yr. old boy with some challenges. He'd been diagnosed with **ADHD, ODD, PTSD**, and **intellectual developmental disabilities.** At that time, I had a 16 yr. old daughter, my miracle child. Even before the adoption, I had a hard time getting the school to give my son the special services he was entitled to so he might have a better chance at succeeding in school. All the meetings led nowhere, just a lot of promises.

I remember the last meeting I had with the school: I sat in the room with just myself and a male counselor. A short while later, another male with a suit came in, then another male with a suit, and then about two more men in suits, and I thought to myself, "all this for one little lady who showed up for the meeting alone, with no real knowledge of the system?"

What they didn't know is that I showed up with mega faith and confidence. Even though they had college degrees and I didn't, even though they were therapist, physiatrist, teacher, principal, and I had no title, I was not intimidated by any of it. What I had was greater than any title or degree, and that was power and authority from the highest.

All this was new to me, though. I never had to take on this kind of challenge before. I didn't understand the jargon being used, and I could barely comprehend the individual education plan that was put in place for my son. The parts I did understand, though, showed me that the services the school district had put in place were not living up to the standard of academic, social and emotional growth that was supposed to have been designed for my child's unique needs.

Most of the people in this meeting I had met with before, either individually or a few at a time. They knew I was a strong advocate for my son, and that I wasn't going away.

Before the next meeting was to occur, I did my research and obtained a parent advocate who taught me what my son should be receiving in order to succeed in the educational system. She taught me what I needed, and showed me how to get it.

In prior meetings, they would give me a little of what my son needed, and hoped it would satisfy me. But at this meeting, it was different. Even with all the suits and their eloquent speech, without fear I let them know where they were lacking on the things that needed to be put in place so that my son could flourish and thrive, which is what the local educational agency is to provide for every student with a disability under the individuals with disabilities education act.

With courage, confidence, and determination, fed up with the school's broken promises and jeopardizing my child's ability to reach his highest potential, explained to them that I needed to see some kind of progress in terms of my son receiving his services within the next few weeks, or I would seek help elsewhere.

Well, as not too much happened in that 2-week time frame, I fulfilled my promise. I hired an education attorney and again found myself in unfamiliar territory with lawyers, psychiatrists, teachers, and other school officials. I did the majority of the talking, advocating for my son; it got a little emotional for me, because it was hard for me to fathom that I had to go this far to get the services my son should have already been given.

Nevertheless, with tears in my eyes, I addressed the individuals sitting in front of me, my attorney at my side, about how my son's basic needs weren't being met. Math, reading, and speech were the subjects where my son fell short, never mind the extra help he needed with social, emotional, and behavioral support.

I explained how, without these services, my son was set up for failure before he even started. I also talked about how the system had failed him numerous times while in foster care for five years, and let them know I wasn't going to allow the system to fail him again. Not on my watch.

After pleading my case and answering a few questions from the school district lawyers, they deliberated for about 45 mins. The lawyers came back, and my son received victory. He received every service available to him educationally, and even monetarily. Lesson to ponder: when you have God at the head, honesty on your side, confidence at your back and courage out in front, you are unstoppable.

The moral of this story is: no matter what you go through, the power, determination, courage, and strength that you possess is stronger than any of the past or even the present pain, struggles, or tragedies you have experienced. Those things don't determine who you are. They are just things that happened. The pain and disappointments may leave some scars, some you can see and some you can't see. Scars can heal, but lessons last a lifetime.

I decided to be a part of this collaborative project because I wanted to share some of my story in hopes it would help someone, even if only in a small way, to know that they're not alone. For me, it was my faith that taught me I can overcome anything. If I am still breathing and trusting in GOD, there is still hope. I can fight and win.

I believe my creator has given me every tool I need to walk through this journey called life, despite the obstacles that may arise.

We just have to be confident in who we are and to fulfill the purpose we were given.

You are strong, you are capable, you are worth more than silver or gold, and you are enough. So go and show up in the world as your authentic self!

To the women who read this chapter and connect with my story: I pray that you may find determination, peace, strength, solace, courage and confidence to be who you were created to be and do the things you were meant to do. Even if you have gone through, or are presently going through some difficult experiences, hurt, pain, or made some unwise decisions, you are not alone! You are an overcomer. Walk in your GOD given power and authority!

If you have gleaned anything from this chapter, I invite you to follow me on my Facebook page (Https://www.facebook.com/kim.-jessup.93) to find out when my solo book "Bruised But Not Broken" will launch. There I go into more details about the events of my life's journey and the trials and tribulations I've overcome.

Stay true to yourself, love yourself, and regardless of what it looks like you can overcome, you can be restored and you are worth it!!!!

"When you find your Purpose, you find your Power."

About the Author

Kimberly Jessup Martin is a servant of GOD. The assistant Pastor of Mt. Zion BBNDC of Philadelphia, she has a resilient heart, and knows one of her assignments in the earth is to exalt, comfort, and uplift those who are hurting. An author, a mother of two adoptive sons, and one beautiful daughter, she has worked for 25yrs. with adults with developmental disabilities, and is an advocate for children with special needs. Kimberly is on SAC (school advisory council), and Ministers the word of GOD Fridays on Facebook. Most importantly she understands that it is the grace and mercy of GOD that has brought her this far and that will continue to manifest the Glory of GOD in and through her life.

https://linktr.ee/Mir1234

#METOOFAMILYCOURTS

REALITY IS STRANGER THAN FICTION

BY LAURA BONETKZY-JOSEPH

What if I told you my incarceration was premeditated without any crime ever being committed? Put in prison with folks sentenced to life for crimes like murder? I'd ask if you'd believe me, but you're just getting to know me, and you're about to discover a snippet of what a woman will do to escape a life of domestic abuse.

Prepare for some cage-rattling: this story is as surreal as it is absolutely true.

Imagine, like a mother bear, you fight for you and your children's freedom from a domestic abuser, only to find yourself put in handcuffs in a courtroom. Ushered off to prison without ever having been accused or convicted of any crime.

Shock sets in.

Newly released from the hospital for severe stress-related cardiac issues, I was scared my ex-husband was going to succeed in killing me at last, while keeping his hands clean… a result of the never-ending perpetuation of abuse permitted to continue monthly for seven years straight without any reprieve after my initial restraining order for protection was granted.

Walking into the courtroom that day, I saw four times the number of court officers present. When threatened with incarceration, I requested my right to a lawyer to be present. As a victim of domestic violence who was experiencing trauma-by-court-system, I could not adequately and appropriately represent myself.

I was DENIED that right.

My father was there that fateful day, and demanded the courts call an ambulance. His request was ignored until he threatened to call the media.

An ambulance arrived 45 minutes later. My blood pressure skyrocketed to dangerous levels with chest pains and heart flutters. I was immediately administered 2 doses of nitroglycerin before arriving at the emergency room; that seemed to stabilize me. There I was, processed and treated by the medical staff like a hardened criminal, ushered away without any treatments, medications, or recommendations for what was happening to me.

Next thing I knew, I was handcuffed behind my back, shoved in the back of a prison transport vehicle, and ushered to Framingham State Penitentiary without any follow-up medical care.

Finger printed. Photographed. Stripped naked in front of corrections officers. Told to bend over while naked, pull my butt cheeks apart and cough. Then marched to my private cell.

Imagine. Your only crime at this point was to leave an abusive marriage to protect your children from further abuse. Doing what the system said to do. Only to end up here, wondering what you did that was so horrific to deserve this life sentence of abuse with impunity.

Unfortunately, my story is not an anomaly. 58,000 children are legally trafficked by way of family courts EVERY year to documented abusers and rapists.

They say abuse often escalates once you leave your abuser, and it did – just not in the way one would think. My ex-husband was really "good at keeping his hands clean" as one police chief told me.

Then the next set of horrors began. I was woken up by prison staff in the middle of the night, getting a fistful of unknown pills shoved down my throat and told to swallow. I didn't know what the medications were. So, the next day I refused these pills, despite the terror of what would happen when I did.

I was then moved to a building shared with approximately 30 other women on bunk beds. This was hard-core prison with inmates like the woman sentenced to life for murdering her landlord. As the story was told to me, she called the police saying she was hearing loud voices in the walls. When the police investigated, they found her landlord's body in between the walls.

My head was spinning in disbelief, as if I were in the Twilight Zone. How could this be real? I racked my brain, struggling with how I got here. I've dedicated my life to service and volunteer work. I'd never hurt anyone. Heck, I didn't want to hurt the man who chose to hurt me and my children. Like so many victims of domestic violence, I begged the police department to not prosecute my ex-husband for assault and battery. I knew only more pain could come of it.

Nine years of marriage. Nine years of what was supposed to be one of the best experiences of my life. I thought I was doing *this* right this time. I thought I was breaking the generational patterns of domestic violence, and I failed miserably... worse than I could ever have imagined.

HOW DID I GET HERE?

Like every little girl with Cinderella fantasies, I played house, dreaming about having the perfect family and career. And when I grew up, I just kept on playing.

I thought I had created the perfect life. I built a successful career in the financial industry. I taught my husband how to be an expert just like myself. An incredible power couple, creating a life together. At least that's what people saw on the surface. Behind the scenes, it was very different.

By the age of 35, I was creating successful financial plans for other families and raising three daughters. I had also filed my first restraining order, in June of 2006. By February of 2007, I was divorced. In September 2007, my ex-husband sought custody, using the system to continue his patterns of control and abuse. And then came the cherry on top: my incarceration.

I constantly questioned how I got here, waking up every morning, wondering if I'd just had the nightmare of nightmares. How could any of what I was living through be real, for real?

We've heard of the term gaslighting before, yes? " *...a form of psychological abuse where a person or group makes someone question their sanity, perception of reality, or memories. People experiencing gaslighting often feel confused, anxious, and unable to trust themselves.*"[1]

My friends no longer recognized me. How did I go from being mega-successful, achieving everything I ever put my mind… to *this*? I was always at the top of my game, highly motivated, outgoing, with an unstoppable award-winning *I-can-do-anything* attitude. I even bought my first home at 19, put myself through college, and was able to save enough money at a young age to fund my retirement. I mean, damm-mmn, I was on track to a good life, right?

After I married, things changed. Mr. Hyde was unleashed. The abuse started out subtle. Suddenly, the cat wasn't allowed here or there. I wasn't permitted to drive without a major argument. I did NOT want to argue. I preferred peace. Meanwhile, my freedom, identity, and power were slowly stripped away as if my life was being erased, shaped and molded like clay into submission.

The jealousy over recognition for my accomplishments enraged him. So much so that he convinced me to turn over my entire client list to him to manage and guilted me into being *"the mother I never had growing up"* to my children. Next he took control and possession of the deed to my home and any other financial assets. I allowed him to, because it was the unselfish, dutiful, loving-wife thing to do. Little did I realize what was actually happening at the time.

Abusers with a premeditated plan carefully orchestrate their execution to avoid detection or suspicion by 3rd parties. By our 6th year of marriage, my husband admittedly shared hotel beds with women half his age, telling me to "get over it; it's just business." Once I came home from the movies with my three daughters to find my husband, sprawled out on the sofa intimately with a woman who—

insult to injury—was wearing *my* pajamas. He claimed what we saw was a figment of my imagination. Ladies, that's a gaslighting 101 tactic.

On top of the ongoing cheating, I was subjected to horrific emotional abuse. I was repeatedly told, for example, that my children would be better off if I were dead, because I was horrible like my mother.

Then came the physical abuse.

The straw that broke the camel's back, made me decide to finally leave? My daughter was accused of stealing money to buy books in first grade. He threatened to have her arrested, thrown in jail, and told her she would never see her parents, sisters, or dog ever again, triggering her to spike a 104-degree fever. This level of threats and trauma to my daughter was ongoing; it ultimately led to the discovery that my seven-year-old was cutting herself.

I started to stand up to him. I thought momma bear could protect her cubs. The submissive me began to find and assert my voice, only to have him grab me by the throat, slam me to the wall or floor, where the threats continued and blackouts ensued.

I found myself losing everything, slowly, one fragment at a time, to this master of masters at the gaslighting game: identity, confidence, friends, career, business, family, assets, home, and savings stripped away. I never even saw it coming.

THE SMOKING GUN OF PREMEDITATION

Two weeks before my incarceration, three things happened simultaneously.

1. I sought a harassment protection order against my ex's lawyer that was well-documented, legally.
2. I was appealing my custody case.
3. We were investigating a corrupt judge.

My children suffered the consequences of my thinking there was freedom from abuse in the USA, governed by rules and laws. I was blinded by faith. Seeker of truth. I didn't see what my actions would cost me, and still cost me to this day.

I always believed the old adage "the truth shall set you free." Until now, I didn't understand what systemic oppression felt like until I was faced with it. There's NOTHING that can compare to the powerlessness you feel when faced with this lack of basic safety and freedom.

So, when I went for the harassment protection order against the lawyer before *another* judge, the lawyer said, "Your Honor, this woman is going to jail in two weeks anyway."

What struck me as odd is, how would this lawyer know I'm going to prison, as if it's a done deal, a matter of fact, unless he's lying, or it's already been pre-arranged with surety? I blogged ahead of time to timestamp this incident, because I know how unbelievable my story sounds.

WHY WAS I SENTENCED TO PRISON?

On paper, the court said I owed $400 in child support. I involved the Department of Revenue (DOR) to take out child support due to the documented and reported countless acts perpetrated against me, including mail fraud, identity theft, insurance fraud, and larceny.

The lengthy history that has been documented with SEC, USPS, IRS, and Police departments was justification to fear access to my banking information. So, when I went before the judge, the money was still pending from DOR, and in transit. Strangely, the judge appeared noticeably upset that I had involved the DOR. I was shocked, because their involvement would have ensured payment of the child support due, ostensibly the reason I was being thrown in jail.

Not only was I sentenced to 30 days in a state penitentiary and my right to a lawyer denied, I was sentenced to criminal court community service four days a week for six months (apparently this was considered just punishment for $400 in child support that was already en route from DOR).

This was strategic. See, I was also trying to start a nonprofit offering pro bono healing services for victims of domestic violence, since what was offered was nonexistent or seriously broken.

On paper, the system supports victims of domestic violence. In reality, it doesn't. Abusers know victims have financial limitations, and will use the system to continue patterns of abuse. It's a legal tactic known as domestic violence by proxy, intended to thwart the efforts of survivors and their advocates toward healing and recovery.

THE REAL REASON THEY PUT ME IN JAIL?

We were investigating the money trail of my prior judge, who ultimately recused himself, admitting bias in my case. We collected 20 solid cases against this judge involving documented child sex abuse and/or domestic violence, and investigating the source of income this judge obtained counseling incarcerated men around child custody. One story that caught my attention was a guy who was incarcerated for dealing, manufacturing, and distributing methamphetamines, who got full custody of his children within 2 weeks after he was released from jail. No supervised visits, full legal and physical custody.

I wanted to know why this judge was going to prisons, mentoring incarcerated fathers on HOW to get custody. Yet, every single victim of domestic violence who went before him seeking abuse protection was denied up to 95% of the time. Meanwhile, documented abusers were given custody, and victims of abuse like myself were denied access to their children for over 10 years. Just when we were getting close to finding the root of the money trail, I was incarcerated.

According to The Prison Reform Trust: a majority of women in prison report having suffered domestic violence, with 53% of women reporting having experienced emotional, physical, or sexual abuse as a child.

I spent $300,000 in legal fees trying in vain to see or speak to my children. I lost my home and business with over a million dollars of calculable damage in 5 years. I was at the brink of homelessness. The only thing my ex didn't succeed at? Collecting on my life insurance policy.

MOVING FORWARD

A lot was triggered when I was incarcerated. However, I also saw it as a blessing, because my eyes were opened to the magnitude of systemic corruption and oppression at play. I was amazed how many women were incarcerated as a legal tactic for abusers to continue patterns of abuse and gain custody. This is how domestic violence by proxy works: if batterers make these women look crazy on paper, well, then, that's just an updated way of saying "she's hysterical" so let's put her in an insane asylum. Classic script straight from the 1944 movie "Gaslight."

A victim can never be free as long as we, as a society, continue to enable the abuser. Remember, if it takes a community to raise a child, then it also takes a community to abuse one. Abusers know how to strip away friends and support structures from underneath you, toying with you like a killer whale does with a seal before the kill.

My friend Elaine had keen insight on what was to come. She threatened to call the police on my ex-husband one day if he didn't leave my home, where he had not resided since he slammed my head to the floor and choked me in front of my children. Afterwards, he threatened her. Later she said, *"Laura, I've dated men from all walks of life, from millionaires to men who were incarcerated with violent pasts, and I've never been more afraid of anyone than your husband. I'm a single mother. I have to think of my daughter's safety. Please do not ask me to testify against him in any way."*

Maybe I am a daydreamer, believing we can change this patriarchal colonialist system that has robbed us of our freedom and power for over 500 years.

When I went to jail, I met women on the inside and listened to their stories. It was validating, yet shocking to learn how many women fell into the grip of addiction only *after* the continued perpetuation of abuse by the system—ignoring allegations of sex abuse, domestic violence, and child abuse.

I went to prison for a cause I believed in, a cause that ultimately cost me custody of my children. Even though I am currently afraid for my safety in sharing my story, I am sharing anyway... because I was silenced. My story needs to advocate not only for my freedom but for that of countless other women who are still NOT free from their abusers. I aim to change this systemic injustice, and shift the culture that allows and supports it.

I still get back up and stand up. I still speak out. I just do it differently. My children will someday know what I have gone through to fight FOR THEM and others like them.

We live in a world that doesn't support women. Our gaslit system is masterful at silencing women, and it is time to change this trajectory that has historically persecuted women for hundreds of years, generation after generation, and STILL does today. Even fame and fortune are no protection, as Frances Farmer, Yoko Ono, Billie Holiday, Britney Spears, and so many others can vouch. I'm here to use my voice to rattle the status quo, and to hopefully inspire others too.

When our voices are silenced, we are not in our full power. We become complicit in a culture of abuse that makes us NOT safe. You deserve to be safe, emPOWERed and using your voice fearlessly. Accessing this power begins with us. Our courage has to be stronger than our fears. We must do that hard inner work and deprogramming, supported by community.

I believe if you can heal trauma, you can heal anything. Currently, we are in the grips of the greatest epidemic we've ever seen, and it is not what you think. We have a culture filled with unresolved, unhealed, unaddressed trauma that can lead to chronic illness, autoimmune disease, mental health issues, and cancer.

While searching to heal the broken me, in my wake, folks sought me out. Since then, I've been supporting survivors of abuse through healing and empowerment as part of my overall mission and work, providing spiritually-based integrative holistic health enrichment since 2006, recently completing my first book on HOW I healed that broken me: *"The Secrets to Healing: An Invitation to Healing Trauma and Other Root Causes of Chronic Illness Using the Japanese Reiki Gokai"*

I am not my story. You are not your story. There is more to us than what happened to us. Together, we can change the ending; turn our triggers into superpowers capable of transforming this toxic, patriarchal system into a safe, equitable system for all humanity.

HOW TO HELP

Here are five things you can do today to help rewrite the culture of abuse:

1. Believe survivors
2. Support whistleblowers
3. Examine our own patriarchal gender biases, known and unknown
4. Teach our children to dismantle this culture of misogyny, abuse, and violence
5. Donate to groups & organizations that support victims of domestic abuse.

To learn more, please check out these FREE resources I put together for you, including the collaborative project *"Triggers & Spiritual Medicine"* here: https://linktr.ee/HealingWithSpirit

About the Author

Since 2006, Laura Bonetzky-Joseph has been providing spiritually based integrative holistic health enrichment with a subspecialty in trauma healing & recovery through workshops, outreach, retreats, and private sessions.

She's an experienced healer, speaker, writer, seeker, social justice junkie, spiritual mentor, intuitive, Jikiden Reiki Shihan (teacher), medicine woman & holistic health professional.

Laura is also a survivor of child abuse, sexual assault, & domestic violence. Over the years, she's become a thought leader and recently launched a collaborative project "Triggers & Spiritual Medicine" on YouTube.

Currently, Laura is enrolled in an addiction counseling certification program at UMass Boston.

Laura's Vision: To break the unrecognized epidemic of unresolved unhealed trauma & create sustainable systems for recovery, healing & empowerment.

Mission: To help others rediscover the power that lies within and to find that treasure buried in the depths of the shadows. To help them become their own superhero.

https://linktr.ee/HealingWithSpirit

DON'T YOU DARE SHRINK

BY DORIANA VITTI

I *tested it, I fought against it, I tried to fit in but no, this is who I am... I'm a cycle breaker.*
When they told me that to write is to step into full vulnerability, I understood it intellectually, but I didn't imagine to this extent.

The vulnerability I discovered in my own words and thoughts and feelings are for the sake of my own wellbeing, and for the wellbeing of other women who need to hear these words.

I write to discover what I know under the layers of what I've been told.

MY SENSE OF SELF

Recently, I punched a man I like… and he laughed.

I started boxing 11 years ago, initially to channel emotional turmoil I wasn't really aware of, due to traumatic family events and the break-up of a long love story. During these same years, I found my sense of belonging in the Ultras movement of my city (soccer supporters not very famous for gentle manners, best known as the hooligans' movement worldwide). I shaved my head, confronting a male-dominated environment, and was determined to carve space to establish myself as equal amongst men mentally, emotionally and physically.

Those were funny days, made of matches in and out of town, loud demonstrations, fighting and violence against opponent fans. Not that I'm proud of everything I've done or believed at that time, but I had the chance to explore some of the deep edges of society, the ones you get to hang around if you feel marginalized, oppressed, exploited, angry and not fitting in your own environment.

I started boxing to channel all of the energy and internal struggle somewhere external, not because I wanted to go around beating people, but because I wanted to make sure no one could beat me. I fell in love with boxing. It was not only a physical activity I was practicing, it became my lifestyle and it was doing something deeply nourishing to my spirit. My days and my routine soon were shaped around my training sessions and resting rhythms, only to get better, only to improve.

My physicality was changing, my self-esteem grew exponentially, my mind was getting forged by the hard training. Finally, I discovered a new control over my emotions I'd never had before. You know, you have no option but to stay focused when you spar with men who weigh 10kg or more than you, who see you as a peer and not a delicate creature to protect. Plus, I was the only woman in the gym for three years.

All of these new gains felt great. What I didn't know was that I was building/reawakening the warrior inside, and this did not come without a cost.

The stronger I got, the more difficult it was for people, especially men, to handle me: my voice, my opinions, the fierceness of my expression and the strength of my body and my spirit.

Although I was going through this journey of visible internal and external growth, some sneaky questions arose from the depths of my subconscious: What if I become *too much*? What if I become too scary? What if I'm not feminine enough? What if it's hard to love me?

And you know what happened? Do you know what happens when we desperately seek to be loved by something that's outside of us? I started shrinking. Although I was growing, I started fearing, I started doubting my voice, even as it was shouting inside. I started doing things differently because if I had done them the way I wanted, then I would have been alone, with no love to turn to. At least, that's what I thought.

So even though I was growing, I shrank. And the fact that men were so scared by my presence made it easier for me to believe I had to adjust my size to fit into a perception of a woman that was way too small for me. All because I was afraid of losing love.

"How does it look when a woman is truly herself?" I asked myself.

My belief was: well, things become very difficult. She'll find herself alone with her strength, she'll grow even wider shoulders in order to carry it all by herself (a thing I was already doing in preparation because I knew I was a lot), she'll be too much, and no one likes handling too much.

With these thoughts in mind, I shrank as I grew.

Do you want to know what happened as a result of this mindest I carried for far too long?

I broke my right knee, and years later I broke my left one.

A plant will break her branches if you put a roof on her whilst she's gloriously growing upward. Likewise, I literally broke my limbs to try to accommodate this contradictory self-direction: grow but shrink.

When we abuse ourselves long enough with thoughts and shoulds that do not reflect our nature, we will eventually end up believing them.

And we'll continuously tell these stories to convince ourselves even more, and to avoid the pain of the truth locked inside.

After a while, I stopped boxing formally, and embarked on different discovery journeys, having lost track of my strong sense of self.

I looked for myself in many places during my spiritual seeking... *what am I?, who am I?...*. I looked everywhere. In my attempt to shrink, I even looked into marriage.

I got married in 2019, to a guy I chased to the point that I moved into his parents' house, first as a friend, then we became a couple.

We married, had a memorable wedding, we were in love, we worked together in the same gym...and the underlying story was still the same: I was diminishing my size.

What if we worked "so well" during these years, only because I was shrinking?

At some point, I got COVID-19. I knew that was not an accident, and that I did not catch the virus only because, you know, *pandemic*. It was not a casual thing. My immune system was already weakened and at its extremes; my emotional body was enduring forced adaptations and induced silences. The air was not allowed to move freely in the lungs of my soul. When I tested positive, I knew there was something deeper I needed to hear, and that Covid was the messenger.

After one month of complete isolation and physical struggle, I recovered and went back to normal life. Nothing had apparently changed around me, nor the situations I left the month before, except that my body at the minimum sign of stress kept sending me symptoms from the just-gone illness.

This is when I actually started listening.

What I heard was a harsh but revelatory truth: I could not keep playing out the same patterns and being the same person in my marriage anymore. The awareness around the long-forgotten and neglected feelings arose stronger and with the days passing I stopped accommodating, I stopped smiling when I meant to be serious, I stopped silencing my anger, and voiced all the issues I had been quietly carrying. I was not roaring strong as many would imagine, but I did not allow quiet acceptance to suffice anymore.

People will never come to understand your needs unless you express them.

There are also people who are extremely emotionally intelligent and do understand even if you say nothing, but they are rare and you shouldn't only rely on them. Learn to express what you need. This comes first.

My marriage fell apart, and the best move when things are falling apart is to stay still and see where they land. I took the leap of faith of doing nothing. You know how hard *that* can be, right? The allowing. I let things play out and speak for themselves, especially my husband's behaviors, choices and actions. Instead of focusing on the potential

I've always seen in him (or maybe hoped he had?) I started watching things as they were, in the moment. The discomfort of not running to fix the situation was unbearable. The shame and the guilt of not doing enough to save the relationship, as if I was the only one in it capable of improvement.

WHEN DOING THE RIGHT THINGS HURTS

We're brought up to think that when we take rightful decisions, we instantly get surrounded by this aura of glory and pride for ourselves. In reality, it depends. There are surely acts of social justice that give us a feeling of empowerment straight away, but it's different when it comes to doing something radical we know needs to change within a relationship we care for, and when we know that an action is right, but it's also going to hurt.

How does it feel not clinging to someone you loved who now wants to leave, or wants different things from what you once wanted together? How does it feel not trying to improve a relationship at all cost when the other person doesn't show the minimum desire to do the same? How does it feel to realize there isn't a guilty party between the two of you, that you are just growing in different directions and maybe have always been at different stages?

Staying still and allowing situations and people to speak for themselves is the right thing to do, but there's no aura of glory that surrounds the events, there's only pain.

Pain for what it was, what could have been, and what has been, for the things we're not trying to repair this time, pain for letting things be what they are, even if they're not clear yet, the dreams we know we can't nurture anymore, pain for this version of ourselves that suddenly feels like they're the only one still standing on a ground that is now shaking. A familiar void opens up, the very void we were trying to a-void when we started shrinking ourselves at the beginning. Beyond that void, we don't recognize anything anymore, and the only thing that keeps us alive and sane is the resilience of our own spirit.

As a woman, culturally especially, I've not been taught to go after my dreams, let alone prioritize them. The fact that I always felt called to do it made me feel so unfit and awkward in my own community. Especially when loved ones did not understand my vision and tried to resize it and me, mainly to evade their own discomfort, and saddled me with labels that felt like a gut-punch. Oof! Right in the desires. The shame and guilt of being called selfish because I wanted to prioritize what I wanted. How many times I felt out of step and hopeless compared to the people around me who seemed to do so well following their scripts meticulously. I had to self-teach and model for myself all the things I wanted to apply, and this did not come without struggles.

Do you know how it feels when you're fully aware that the parts of you that used to constitute your identity, created by your family, culture and environment, aren't serving you and need to die?

The pain of rebirthing yourself is real.

And also temporary.

WALKING AWAY...

Leaving hasn't been as dramatic as I thought it would be. My ex-husband and I both knew our relationship was shifting, and that although we cared deeply for each other, our life seasons were out of sync. In the end, we both recognized that what mattered most was respecting and honoring each other's journeys and attempts at fulfilling our visions for life and for ourselves.

I left peacefully, and we continue to support each other's transition.

I went back to the gym recently and I rediscovered the strong woman I once loved being.

Remember that man I liked, who laughed when I punched him? We were sparring at the gym, and I threw a punch instinctively, something neither of us was expecting in that combo. But rather than upsetting or angering him, my moxie surprised and delighted him. Do you know what that taught me? That the right people will get me, and will stay. No matter what. That I will never, ever be *too much* for those who truly belong in my life.

In October of 2021, I flew to Medellin, Colombia, following the desire to create something valuable for myself, and to build a road that had not been trodden by anyone in my family other than myself. Aside from my father, from whom I inherited the strong need for adventure and discovery, no one in the community of people in my small home town in the South of Italy can understand the desires my heart craves, and now I can say "that's okay." Taking this physical distance and space was just what I needed to bring me to a place where I know I don't need to explain or justify what I want to anyone other than myself.

It can be a pretty lonely journey sometimes, decisive choices are not always easy to live with, but we can surely not live without them.

I have rented my own pretty, small, and cozy apartment. Many lovely plants are on the balcony and around the house, I decorated it as I like, and it's now the safe and welcoming space I needed. As publishing manager, I'm doing a job that I love, working side-by-side with many women on their own journeys of self-discovery, and with my friend and colleague Sierra Melcher, founder of Red Thread Publishing.

Do I know anything about what's coming next? No, I don't. I'm still dropping layers and layers of overgrown skin I didn't realize was hanging off the edges of my psyche. Sometimes I'm mad at myself for how much I shrank, and for the life I contributed to creating prior to this; for all the time I spent, for the fights I put myself into, and the tears I cried. How many hot tears ran down my face sitting in my bed alone, in such pain that I was numbed and waited for something to take me. How many times I considered suicide when no one was hearing my voice, when all I really needed was to hear my own voice!

I know that all I did and didn't do was to keep me safe and protected when I needed it, and that I did my best to the best of my abilities and understanding. The woman into whom I'm growing now has a deeper sense of safety in herself, a deeper trust in life, and while she's building healthy boundaries, she keeps her heart wide open.

These days, I dedicate love songs to myself: *Jealous Guy* by John Lennon, and Jake Wesley Rogers' cover of *I'll stand by you*. There's no turning back this time, I can only move forward.

Keep believing in the voice that speaks from the depth of your soul; she is the guide, and she'll carry you through.

Grow, and do not shrink.

About the Author

Doriana Vitti, Publishing Manager at Red Thread Publishing, supports women to get their stories out into the world, with the mission to make a global impact and uplift all of humanity. Her innate empathy and compassion for the human soul and mind makes it easy for her to read between the lines of people's words and feel their emotions, gifts she employs to empower the world around her, helping others find their true desires and voices. In her free time, you can find her training at the gym or walking outside, connecting with nature.

https://linktr.ee/DorianaVitti

MISS UNDERSTOOD

BY TOBI K. MARES

"Ruin is a gift. Ruin is the road to transformation."

— ELIZABETH GILBERT

Feisty feels like a term to describe an aged and seasoned woman who wears flashy clothes, cusses with no care, and drinks whiskey whenever she wants to. She is full of opinions and wisdom with a certain resolution towards life. She has made friends with all the bullshit and dominated anything that got in her way. Feisty feels uncomfortably honest, yet assertively benevolent. Making no apologies for owning the struggles and winning the internal battle. Some people roll their eyes at her, some laugh and tell tales about her legacy… pretending to have had a front row seat in her experiences.

I was a tomboy. Ran around the neighborhood with no shirt on as a little girl. Crawled through sewer lines and played in the creek. I climbed trees. Once, tornado sirens were blazing, and I was riding my bike home but I heard a little kitten crying. I jumped off my bike and climbed a massive pine tree to save the kitten. I hid kitty in my closet for days before my mom found out, but I got to add her to our flea collection.

We used to role play TV shows in the neighborhood, and I always wanted to be a big-boobed blonde from BJ and the Bear who needed to be saved by the boys. My boy gang ruled Glenview Drive. I would pick on other girls and pull them by their braids. I was a bully but full of sensations of deep undefined sadness. When I was alone I would play dolls and cry for my mom. She was 30, divorced and worked two jobs to support two daughters.

My mom worked at the best restaurant in town on weekends. This is where she met Duane. The 19-year-old black cook. Nobody could cook a steak like Duane, and never did a customer send one back.

He moved in with us. Gift.

In the early 80's this was the perfect storm for all the hate and racism. I was called n***** lover at school. I had a family member who would sit outside of our house and spy on the black man living at our house, to report back to my dad's family, or whoever would listen to her diabolical and drug-induced diatribes. A hair salon in my town has always been the center of the feeding trough for the gossipers. Do they not know how painful their gossip is to others?

Feisty, I think not. Wretched, more like..

My mom would make Duane duck down in the car when we passed someone she knew. This broke my fucking heart. I knew it was wrong. I loved Duane so much. When my mom was done with him, she traded him in for a real live redneck. I found this out when I came home from a sleepover one day, and there was a moving truck in the driveway, moving us to his house, just as I was about to turn 13. As we left Glenview Drive, my home for 12 years of life, the cats had disappeared. Years later, we realized Dave took them to the "dairy farm," which meant he shot them.

My rebel yell really echoed through the dilapidated town as a teenager. I was mean to teachers, got attention from ridiculous pranks, D's and F's, detentions all the time, the pot smoking, the sneaking out, the shoplifting, and skipping school. The most damaging, though, was my cooperative and non-confrontational disposition. I was a guy's girl. The boys were all drawn to that tomboy side of me. Of course, I did break most of the fashion rules, wearing things no other girls would wear. Cool stuff, like men's button-down tux shirts with rhinestone necklaces. You know, a little bit leather and a little bit lace. I never followed trends, unless I was moved to try extra hard to fit in.

With my circle of girlfriends, I was there to provide comic relief, the lead goofball, I knew where all the parties were, had the best pot, and usually had the ulterior motives of where the boys are. I could concoct any escapade with my nickname MacGyver.

I was too timid to ever say no to the pressures and buried my voice. Whether it was to try some cocaine, watch 10 hours of The Simpsons and fake laugh, go on life threatening rides on dirt bikes, or have sex. I had no voice. I call it my 'scared little girl syndrome.' Wanting to be loved but never wanting to rock any boat.

It was no surprise to anyone that I dropped out of high school and got arrested at 17 for pot. In my own complacency, I took the blame for most of the pot that belonged to my guy friend. Then I was put on supervision, which I violated by running into my probation officer… who first hit on me, then filed the violation when that didn't end in his favor. I voluntarily went to jail for 30 days, rather than suffer through more probation in a broken system. I then became a mother at age 19.

Never mind rocking the boat: I blew that shit up.

My personal learning style is through repetition, so I repeated the picking. Picking abusers, cheaters, alcoholics. My life was just a constant loop of chaos. Chasing public aid, chasing jobs, chasing my alcoholic cheater, chasing money, but literally dying for serenity. Underneath it all, I was taking one step towards "better." Those small movements were far overshadowed by the daily dramas. I knew this was not the life I wanted or was supposed to be living; however, I knew it was the choices I was making. I accepted my suffering, never really blaming anyone but myself. Ruin.

"I got my GED with the highest score in the state!"

"She's a high school drop out with only a GED; she'll never amount to anything."

"I enrolled in classes at the community college and there is a daycare on site!"

"She is sucking off the government and getting free childcare."

"My boyfriend put my head in the wall and I have a bad concussion, at the hospital, can you pick me up?"

"You made your bed, now lie in it."

And so, I did. I would have rather killed myself numerous times, real contemplation, then ask someone for help, from all the guilt, shame, and abandonment I felt. I felt ruined for a very long time. I continued to chip away at my schooling, while simultaneously staying in abusive relationships. I continued to have children and not get married. I continued to move in search of either a better opportunity, to live in a safer place, or to escape my domestic violence qualifier. I moved a lot. Nobody likes to move. It is one of the hardest things to do. Especially with children and alone. It was something I had to choose in the continued baby steps towards something better. In reflection, I should have sat still in some situations, but I was in a constant state of fight or flight.

I was not scared to work, and I did the work… I worked jobs not many women would do. I crawled through shit-filled vats, laid next to smashed rats, worked in black carbon rooms (had carbon coming from my pores for a year after I quit). I was a certified welder, thanks to my dad for giving me an opportunity at his industrial construction company. I only wished he paid me fairly.

I took this craft and went to work for CAT- as the first female welder they had hired in 20 years. I was good, too. Skillful. I would weld and be lost in my thoughts. I kept a mini composition book in my flannel pocket. I would create stories in my head, take notes, and write them in journals. I loved to write, and my imagination and creativity was constant. This got me into trouble many times in my life. People always wanted to know what was in my journal. What is on the pages? From being a little girl with a Hello Kitty diary, and my sister reading it to my mom, my step-mom taking it in high school to make xerox copies for the family, to jealous boyfriends going into a rage and screaming inches from my face. It felt like the most humiliating and most disloyal act.

Once my boss at CAT had harassed me out of my job... remember the character Harlan in Thelma and Louise??? That was my boss, Dwight. I quit, left my trade behind, all because of this dick. I went to work for Southwest Airlines as a flight attendant. I had my sights set on finishing my college degree and working in corporate.

Once I had finally had enough suffering in my life, my brain innately looked down the road ahead... GOALS. However, my roads often had every obstacles, falling rocks, sharp turns, rough terrain, steep grades, dead ends, and many times, I was going the WRONG WAY. I kept on.

My job as a flight attendant was unrealistic as a single mom of 2 and little help. I knew it wasn't going to be long term but just getting through the short term was insurmountable. Babysitters for 4 days at a time. Commuting with a 3-hour drive to Chicago and a 4-hour flight to Phoenix, just to get to my base. Moving to Phoenix to be closer to work, only to afford a horrible little apartment, and struggle to pay babysitters. Being stuck in a city due to severe sinus infections, leading to sinus surgery. A 2-year-old son who had unexplained monthly fevers of 106 and higher, in and out of emergency rooms. Holy shit. Thinking about it makes my eye twitch. Quit.

I moved back to my hometown, desperate to be out of the sky and on the ground. Any life would feel like a piece of cake after that 3-year stint.

I was accepted into a private college, Millikin University, something I often wished but never thought I would ever be good enough. When I enrolled in their accelerated adult program, a wonderful thing for adults, I literally left and thought to myself, I will never finish. Preemptive RUIN. I expected my own failure, constantly. At this point, I had bought my first house and on my own, thanks to all the irresponsible mortgage lenders in 2003, I made it into the bubble.

I had not had a relationship in several years, and I literally picked the biggest alcoholic in a room of 100. It was the missing piece in my mind. I was finally stable, building a life, owned a home, getting a college degree, and I wanted a partner. A family. It did not take me long to realize that my patterns were still going strong. Three years and one last moment of fearing for my life... and that was that..

I began working at a restaurant part time and worked a day job. I was going to school 6 pm- 10 pm twice a week, slowly chipping away at my degree. I had to take time off to rebuild from the latest implosion and get out of my depressive state. While I was still being threatened by my ex, for the grand finale in life lessons.... enter the narcissist. They are first a hero, they help, then they groom, groom, groom, until they have you. Then it is your worst nightmare.

This relationship produced two more babies for me, and psychological abuse I can't explain. I have tried explaining this phenomenon time after time. Unless you've experienced it, you won't get it. The physical and sexual abuse, I won't get into. These two daughters kept me alive, because I was a wonderful nurturer and I HAD to stay alive, or he would be raising them. My two older children did not get the best version of me during this time, and you know, mom guilt like no other. I was just trying not to commit suicide, for years.

I left the narcopath, just after the birth of baby 2. Knowing all the embarrassment that came along with that decision, from people who did not know who he really was/is. RUIN.

Somewhere in there was an ember. Buried under the years of guilt, shame, failure, embarrassment, pain, suffering, abuse, poverty, debt, came a little flicker to keep on keepin on. A path not so crooked and not a dead end, but quite literally, endless. It was my road to transformation.

Not even my children could repair my broken soul. The only thing that truly saved me was Nichiren Daishonin's Buddhist practice. Just like I picture my hero, Tina Turner, fellow Buddhist member, and sister in trauma, I would sit at my altar feeling absolute ruin, and absolute desperation. Chanting Nam-myoho-renge-kyo, for hours, days, weeks, and years, provided me with clarity and serenity. I stopped seeking what I wanted outside of myself and knew it was all within.

I made my declaration. In six detailed pages, I declared exactly how I wanted to see my life, my home, my success, my community and my partner. I would accept nothing less, even if it meant I live my life alone, I will do so happily. The burn in the vortex of my soul was heard by the Universe. I was delivered my loving husband, and a massive shift in circumstances. When I packed up the U-Haul and pulled out of that fucking hell I was in, he delivered me to peace on Earth. Heaven in a little community in Indiana. He gave us a life and love, just as I had imagined in my declaration.

Some of my struggles still remain. I am still riddled with the remnants of CPTSD: deep-seated anger, frequent nightmares and flashbacks, anxiety, tendency to withdrawal or self-sabotage, avoidance, physical bouts with full-body tension, irritability, inability to feel joy, at times numb, and guilt and shame to last ten lifetimes. This impacts everyone around me. The geographical cure and the loving husband does not change the biology of my traumatized brain. An overactive amygdala and underactive prefrontal cortex is my current state.

There is work to be done. I know it. Transformation never ends. Change never ceases.

 "Human beings are inherently endowed with the power to bring the best possible results from the worst possible circumstances"

— DAISAKU IKEDA, PRESIDENT OF THE SOKA GAKKAI
INTERNATIONAL

My feistiness has been misunderstood not only by me, but by everyone who knows me, thinks they know me, or had chats about me while getting their "Speak to the Manager" haircuts at the salon. We are all entitled to have our journeys, and mine has been tough, non-traditional, and at times, scandalous. But, you can quote me on this: "Two tears in a bucket, fuck it."

I make no apologies to anyone, unless I have wronged them. I have wronged myself more than anyone else, that I promise. I am now an aging and seasoned woman, who wears mechanic suits with pink bows and flashy shoes. I cuss a shit ton. I prefer a filthy martini with 3 blue cheese olives. I have an opinion about everything, but choose not to share. I have been uncomfortably honest, even when others successfully recast it as a lie. Feisty now feels like not giving up in the face of monsters and fighting for better. It is the courage to share my whole story and owning it, with less guilt or shame. Being aware of my flaws, and hoping those who love me can be blessed with higher tolerance and stronger compassion.

Feisty is my continued effort to be successful and financially independent, just so I can share with others. Making gutsy moves when others doubt my ability. Shutting up the voice of "I can't" that keeps me awake at night. Owning my entrepreneurial spirit and tipping the balance of determination over fear. I have had a lot of jobs with many underlying goals. I have the benefit of always being able to say, "I did that."

Feisty is boldly and bravely fighting to heal anger, or to show it. I am feisty enough to forgive a mutha fucka.

I am on the verge of opening my food business, finishing my novel, and trying to earn some doll hairs with my cute little e-commerce biz. I am an expert in going after it… and I must be feisty enough to forgive myself if that were to become another curve in the road.

Feisty is honoring all that hardship and recognizing I was still able to dream and be creative.

Feisty is to focus on the feats and not the failures. I AM ALIVE. I have survived. I am always working towards THRIVE.

As my feisty Mother in Law says, "I've never had a boring day in my life!" Hear! Hear! All those choices, all those paths, all the suffering, is the gift.

About the Author

In addition to the school of hard knocks, Tobi graduated from Millikin University with a Bachelor's degree in entrepreneurship and business leadership, and a Master's in human services counseling and life coaching. Look for her upcoming book, "Goodness Gracious: A memoir of a woman who transcends from hardship, suffering and abuse by means of food, love and entrepreneurship." An expert in overcoming massive obstacles, loving others for their flaws, and being open to sharing her own, Tobi's one wish is for there to be more love than hate.

https://linktr.ee/iloveGoodnessGracious

WRITING MY OWN RULES

BY HALLIE AVOLIO

My husband, Paul, and I were driving to my best friend, Pam's, 40th birthday. I was wearing the cutest hot pink lace mini-dress. Tears were rolling down my face.

"Dammit! I don't want to smudge my mascara!" I cried.

Paul passed me a tissue. I blotted under my eyes, keeping the mascara intact.

"Can I really do this?" I asked him.

"Babe, you can do anything you want to do."

It was that moment that I realized he was right. I COULD do anything I wanted to do.

I COULD DO ANYTHING I WANTED TO DO!

As if that statement was the key I needed to unlock the shackles that had been holding me back for nearly 40 years.

For 40 years I followed the rules.

The BORING rules.

Not surprising, as a first-born daughter to first-born parents. My brother was born 7 years later; the large age gap was by design. My parents believed that if they had their kids further apart in age, our generation wouldn't experience the same torturous sibling rivalry they had experienced. Plus, life would be easier because my parents would never have two kids in diapers at the same time.

So, there I was, in my earliest formative years, the lone kid in a family of adults. No siblings, no cousins. Just adults. Talking about adult things. Expecting me to entertain myself, play quietly, and to "be a good girl."

I took my job VERY seriously. I had to be the BEST at this good girl persona. If anyone could get a gold star for being a good girl, it was ME.

When my brother was born, there was a new expectation attached to my job description: Second Mom. At 7 years old, I was thrilled! I had a real-life baby to play with and take care of. Just like my favorite doll. I changed diapers and fed him and got up with him when he cried on weekend mornings so my parents could sleep in. As I got older, I stayed home to babysit while my parents went out on date nights. I played with him, made him meals, and put him to sleep some nights. I was an excellent Second Mom. NAILED IT. Definitely worthy of at least 2 gold stars.

At first, I didn't have any problem with this. But when I got to high school, I began to get resentful of the Second Mom role. I wanted to go out with my friends on the weekends and my parents said no. They said I had to babysit so they could go out on date night. What choice did I have? Inside, I was stewing, but my allegiance to being a good girl was much stronger. I justified my dissatisfaction by accepting the $20 they paid me to babysit.

There are many perks to being a gold-star bearing good girl/rule follower. I was allowed to be independent and was never grounded. My parents never questioned my friendships, and when I asked for something, I almost always got it.

The downside, however, is that when I got a taste of rebellion, I would often take it too far. I couldn't distinguish the difference between asserting my own authority and acting self-destructively. I remember a pivotal moment in 6th grade when my self-destruction really got me into trouble and threatened my good girl status.

I was falsely befriended by two popular girls who thought I was the perfect scapegoat for their mean girl energy.

"Come on Hallie, this will be fun! Just take this stick of deodorant and rub it all over her locker. No one likes her anyway."

I took the stick of Solid White Secret, Baby Powder Fresh scent, and smeared it all over the outside of the other girl's P.E. locker. Something stirred inside of me. Like kindling for a fire that is ready to take off. I had never felt this exhilarated, and it was the first time Victoria revealed her power to me.

Victoria is my inner rebel. She can be a real bitch, so I have to watch out for her shenanigans.

When Mrs. Avery, the P.E. teacher, found me at the lockers holding the evidence in my hand (caught white-handed!), she marched me straight to her office. Somehow, while I was fueling Victoria's fire, the two mean girls disappeared, and I was left with no one to blame but myself. I got 2 days detention for that stunt and I remember being so embarrassed as I told my parents.

Fortunately, since I was mostly a good girl, my parents figured the detention was enough punishment and they didn't ground me.

That's how my life went along for almost 40 years. I spent 98% of the time following the rules and collecting gold stars. I was always a good student, and when I graduated UCLA with honors, I got a great job for a Fortune 100 corporation doing business to business sales. I married my college sweetheart and we bought a condo, adopted a rescue dog (a black and white chihuahua we named Rocco), and we had 3 kids by the time I was 35.

Do you know how exhausted I was managing that life and those expectations for nearly 4 decades? Forget about keeping up with the Jones'... I couldn't keep up with ME. Endless mornings of snoozing until the very last second when the cries of "Mom! Mom! Mom!!!" yanked me out of bed and made me want to strangle someone or crack open a bottle of Sauvignon Blanc (I have never been a Chardonnay girl).

I was Bill Murray in *Groundhog Day*. This is my life? Again and again and again? Ugh.

What happened to my fucking dreams and my goals and my vision of being this high-paid corporate executive sitting in a plush corner office? Clearly I traded that in for supporting my husband and his entrepreneurial dreams, my three kids and their incessant demands, all so that I could follow some stupid rule book that I never want to read in the first place.

Victoria was stirring again.

When my oldest son was born, I left the corporate world so I could split my time between helping my husband in his small IT business and raising our kids.

My Second Mom experience gave me the confidence boost I needed to take on this momentous task of raising tiny humans (a whole other world when they are your own kids!). And working for my husband Paul felt like the "right choice for our family" because I had business skills he didn't, and I could help him build his business. Gold-star bearers always make the "right choices."

All the while, Victoria's rebellion was getting harder to ignore. Following the rules felt more and more stifling. I pushed that energy down like squashing a cardboard box to fit in the recycling bin. Yet, the more I pushed it down, the more it wanted to pop up and take over my entire being.

Working for my husband felt like the biggest chore. I hated going into the office. I spent more and more time avoiding doing anything productive and instead spent my time surfing Facebook and visualizing my escape.

Taking care of my kids was not much better. I loved my children, but everything they did bugged the shit out of me. My patience was non-existent and I was always on my phone either texting or scrolling.

I can't tell you how many family movies I missed because I spent 90% of the time hunched over my phone instead of being engaged with what the rest of my family was doing. And I would make play dates with other moms so that we could leave the children in another room to play while we would drink cocktails between 10AM and 1PM before we had to leave to put our kids down for nap times.

The biggest problem was that I had no idea what I wanted. Truth be told, I had never given myself permission to ask this basic and essential question.

What do I want?

And the thing is, even if I had asked at that point in time, I would have come up empty. Because I had no fucking idea.

To take it even further, my inner rule-follower was struggling because there truly were no rules to follow at this stage in the game. It was impossible to get a clear answer when Googling "What do I want?"

And each time I would try something that might make me happy or bring me joy like a new volunteer position or interviewing for a potential job, I came up even more disgruntled.

Paul would ask, "Babe, why are you looking for a job? Do you really want to work for someone else and have no freedom? You will completely give up your flexibility. We will have to put the kids in daycare, and all the money you earn will just go to pay for it. Is that REALLY going to make you happy?"

NO!

I felt like SCREAMING!!!!

"No, it won't make me happy! I just want to live my life and figure out what the hell I want, but I don't know what that is and I'm so angry and frustrated!"

Of course, I didn't actually say that. I just nodded and agreed and swallowed that resentment and frustration. Victoria was fuming, but what could I do? I had no choice.

That's what I thought. I truly believed I had no choice. I was the victim in my own life and I had made bad choices and now I had to live with it. I was no longer a good girl collecting gold stars. I was a victim who couldn't think of anything she wanted more than to escape and wake up in a new reality. I put on a fake smile as I got the kids ready for school. I forced myself to do work I didn't want to do. And I drank a LOT of wine (I knew all the best Sauvignon Blancs at Trader Joe's). I thought the wine would solve the problems I had brought on myself.

There were many low points. Like the time I was so drunk at my daughter's first soccer practice I could barely see straight, and my husband had to drag me to the car until practice was over and then put me in bed when we got home. Or the time I got paralyzed with fear when I saw my reflection in the mirror on the way to the beach and I literally couldn't move my body while my kids yelled, "Mommy! Mommy! When are we going?"

Looking in the mirror, all I could see was failure. Failure to take care of my body... do you see those belly rolls, double chins, and ALL THE cellulite? Failure to be a good parent... my kids are screaming and crying in the other room and I literally can't move. Failure to do anything professionally successful because my husband's business wasn't booming and I was in charge of sales. Failure to make enough money to go on vacations. Failure to afford a bigger house that didn't make me feel claustrophobic. Failure, failure, failure.

Victoria had taken the wheel and slammed her stilettoed foot on the gas. Victim mentality, self-destruction, and self-sabotage were all I could do. I was not in survival mode. I was in toxic self-destruct mode.

And yet, I kept digging myself deeper and deeper. They say our brains get comfortable, even when the comfort zone is toxic. My comfort zone looked like a combination between an alcohol induced haze, stuffing empty calories into my face, excuses about why everything sucked, and picking fights with the people I was supposed to love the most.

Hallie the gold-star-bearing good girl had fully given way to Victoria the rebel. One of the worst nights of my life, I remember going to sleep (or rather passing out) next to my husband, only to wake at 2AM to him pacing the room.

"Where are you going?" I asked through sleep-filled fogginess.

"I'm leaving." He said.

Still half-asleep and probably hung over, I was so confused. "Where are you going? Why are you packing a bag?"

"I can't do this anymore. I can't do *us* anymore. I can't be yelled at and looked at like I'm the person who ruined your life. I don't know what to do anymore but I can't do this. I'm leaving."

PANIC MODE!

Shut the fuck up Victoria, Hallie is coming back.

I begged him to stay. I cried. I told him I would be better. I told him I didn't want him to go, even though every action I had taken for the last year would indicate otherwise.

"You can't leave me! You can't leave me! No no no!!! I will fix this. I will fix this. I will figure it out and I'll get better. I promise."

I don't know if it was the tears or the fact that you should never make decisions at 2AM that prompted him to stay, but he did. And I did intend to get better. But as soon as morning came around, Victoria rolled back in with her black leather jumpsuit and Louboutin stilettos and said "this is my show."

Consciously, I knew something had to give and something had to change. I knew that things were not good in my marriage, or with my kids. I knew that I didn't have a career of my own where I could find success and feel good about my accomplishments. But subconsciously, I was in a vicious cycle that felt impossibly hard to break free from.

It's amazing how sometimes the smallest moments will be the massive catalyst for the change we need in our lives. Although it would seem that my husband nearly leaving me would wake me up and make me see the faults in my ways, that event only gave Victoria permission to activate her "fuck you" energy. You want to leave me? Fuck you! No way! I'll show you how this is going to go down. We went on like this for a few more months.

The actual moment that brought me to my knees was when I was finally able to SEE myself in the mirror of a dressing room in a boutique with horrific lighting. Just a few months after that dark night with Paul, I was searching for a dress to wear to my mom's birthday dinner. I was exhausted and depleted and had absolutely no idea who I was or what I even looked like. I tried on dress after dress, pants, skirts, blouses... and none of them fit. How could clothes 2 sizes too small fit on this beat up body? I stared myself down in that mirror and although Victoria wanted to be the boss, Hallie started to break through.

But of course, no good breakthrough comes without a breakdown.

In that mirror, I saw all the shame, the anger, the resentment, and the embarrassment. I cried. Correction: I UGLY CRIED. And I called Paul and I yelled at him for no reason. And I came home and paced in my room. My stomach was in knots. I cried. I thrashed. I was literally breaking out of the pain that I had inflicted on myself over the past 2 years. I was breaking through a lifetime of desperately trying to get more gold stars.

That was the simple moment that changed my life forever. Because once I quit thrashing like a wild animal caught in the chase, I felt a sense of calm and peace that I hadn't felt in as long as I could remember. I knew in that moment I could make the choice to be a better person and allow Hallie to come back to life and allow Victoria to take a much-needed vacation.

Over the next 6 months I did a deep dive on ME. Since Hallie was back, I activated gold-star mode and took action quickly to rebuild. And this time... with my OWN rule book!

I went to therapy and started reading personal development books. I listened to countless hours of podcasts on mindset and self-love. I started to journal and think about my dreams (I had never thought of those before!). I learned about affirmations and how when you really embody the words of your mantras, you can feel them shift your energy in your body. I did a workout/nutrition program and lost the 30 pounds that had piled on during Victoria's reign.

By the time Paul and I were driving down to my best friend's 40th birthday party, I was feeling better than ever about our marriage, my parenting skills, and most importantly ME. And when he encouraged me that I could do anything I wanted to do, the thing I wanted to do was become a manifestation and self-love coach so I could help other women find their own path to self-love and freedom and manifesting their wildest dreams (Use my Ultimate Manifestation Guide e-book to help you on this journey - link at end).

You are reading this book collaboration because something in you was drawn to our common theme of being feisty. What does feisty mean to you? To me, feisty is about showing up in your life the way YOU choose to show up. It's an energy of knowing that you are absolutely worthy of acting in alignment with what is most important to you because you value it in your mind, heart, body, and spirit.

Since 2020, we have been in a collective energy of revolution and breaking free from old narratives and ways of being. The Victorias of the world have been given permission to go on a time-out and the rest of us have started to dust ourselves off and get to work. Self-love is a choice you make daily. And when you stand in your power and understand that this is YOUR LIFE, the love for yourself increases momentously.

My intention in writing this chapter is that you really begin to dig deep and ask yourself three essential questions:

Who am I? What do I want? What is my purpose?

And as you peel back the layers and honor yourself with the answers, you allow your feisty-side to be free.

About the Author

Hallie Avolio is not a *typical* anything... that includes woman, mother, friend, entrepreneur, or coach. Hallie is an affirmation queen, a lover of core values, and is obsessed with empowering women to create a life they love that is Sassy As F*ck.

Through her manifestation and self-love coaching, Hallie utilizes many modalities to help women connect to their greater purpose and their highest Self. She loves to help women get unstuck, find self-love, manifest their purpose, and live this life to the fullest.

She is the Founder & President of Sassy Healthy Fit, an organization created with the mission to teach as many humans as possible to love themselves unconditionally and create a "F*CK YES LIFE!", and to make this world a brighter place through each of our unique gifts.

https://beacons.ai/sassyhealthyfit

Ultimate Manifestation Guide:

https://mailchi.mp/sassyhealthy.fit/manifest

A RECIPE FOR ALCHEMIZING OUR EMOTIONS TO HEAL

BY CRYSTAL GRENIER

As women, we don't give ourselves time to alchemize. I want to use my experience as an alchemy: a transformation of emotional processing to create better health, free from disease.

I offer a portal to move the darkness of illness into the light of energy to realize abundant, healthy living.

APPETIZERS - FEED TO NOURISH EMOTION

From my emotional birth of forced pull into this world, my childhood continued to unfold with tragedy and heartbreak. My young father was killed in an airline accident shortly after I turned two. This life-altering experience moved my mom and infant brother into an unexpected plan and place of living.

This new "normal" forced our family dynamic of three into years of unhealthy negative stepfamily drama experiences (my mom remarried twice before her passing last year). The years of growing up in this environment silenced me, compounded my unprocessed grief, and had me secretly craving physical and emotional paternal love and affection, which led me to make questionable choices.

Another tragic death happened in 1986. My half-sister was killed in a car accident at 17. This event, of course, impacted our family again, this time with more heart wrenching punch, and included other members of our extended family.

This unstable home front groomed me to consistently take control while cultivating my high achieving, conflict-avoidant, type-A personality.

My emotional plate served up an overflowing meal of negative, self-deprecating, lack of self-love and a yearning for affection and approval. As a child, I was a quick study to do what was expected without being asked or told to avoid conflict and backlashing. I kept all words and thoughts to myself, and rarely shed a tear even though on the inside, I was hurting and angry. I was secretly craving affirmation, praise, some type of tangible acknowledgment of acceptance.

My emotions were being nourished in a negative way. I was absorbing all the external chaos, negative dynamics, and backlash of an emotionally and mentally abusive stepfather. My mother was so passive she rarely stood up for herself, let alone my brother and me.

I externally strove to define my identity and my craving for affection through team sports, academics, other social circles, and my close friends' families.

As I continued this emotional overeating acceleration into my young adult life, I was living a life of constant partying, seeking male companionship for all the wrong reasons, job-hopping, constantly bouncing like a ball from one thing to another, reaching without a hold onto something or someone to bring me happiness, stability and joy.

Through these years of unlearned and untaught nutrition to feed my emotions with healthy healing, I was slowly growing disease.

In the summer of 2017, my disease manifested itself in the form of a lump under my right armpit. Dr. Google suggested cancer on more than one visit to many sites. After an ultrasound and biopsy, the verdict was in: I had Invasive Ductal Carcinoma, aka breast cancer.

At first, I felt like I had been handed a death sentence: I have cancer, it will spread, and I am going to die. Disbelief, despair, sadness, then anger overwhelmed me before sharing the news with family and friends.

Once I accepted the reality of having cancer, I stepped back into my familiar role of control to take action steps towards getting rid of the disease so I could focus on continued healing.

The two-month waiting period from diagnosis to surgery was a brutal challenge of patience. After surgery and during treatments, my emotions were up and down like a roller coaster. Up, down and all around.

I can't go back and change my past, but I can be present to nourish my future.

Physically, our body can harbor many emotions that may surface like an itchy rash that we can't scratch enough. We may feel like someone super heavy is sitting on top of us, crushing our chest. Or like all our joints have decided to throw an aches-and-pains party. We may struggle to breathe, feeling dizzy, anxious and depressed. There is no energy to give to anyone, not even ourselves.

Mentally, our mind takes over with memory loss, mood swings, maybe outbursts of anger, lack of temper control, feelings of regret from a wavering decision, and wait, oh yeah, I almost forgot, forgetfulness.

Our emotional intelligence, or EQ, may be lacking. We may not understand how to use and manage our emotions in positive ways to relieve our stress, communicate effectively, empathize with others, overcome challenges and defuse conflict.

Belief in a higher good or divine being or whatever that icon of worship is for you, will bring you what you ask for. Spiritually, our prayers and blessings of healing will feed our emotions with something bigger and grander than our being.

Can we talk about eating for a sec?

Okay, so another important component to feeding our emotions comes in the form of physical consumption of tangible carbs, protein and fats. Are we choosing options to feed our cells healthy calories to promote and encourage healing?

Cancer and its relation to food intake have a whole new feeling for me. My choice to cut out foods and drinks that don't make me feel good and aren't continuing to support my healing is my choice. I realized I needed to eat to heal, not eat to hurt.

Food can be comforting. We eat to soothe our negative emotions; fear, anger, stress, boredom, sadness or loneliness. A loss of a loved one or the daily hassles of life can trigger our emotional eating to pull us into a downward spiral. Or do we not eat at all? An internal struggle for control of the self calls for an external acceptance or persona. We are feeding our cells to promote emotional self-harm which in turn may increase chances of internal ailments and/or disease.

Intuition is your nutrition! Pay attention to what you are feeling when you prepare and eat a meal. What mood you are in, and why are you eating it in the first place? Is it to satisfy your hunger, or to comfort an emotion? Listen to the emotion and feel into its growl. Then make a healthy choice in how to feed it.

Being present and conscious of our thoughts, feelings and behaviors and how we are feeding them is key to living better with our chronic illness and/or maintaining a disease-free lifestyle.

MAIN COURSES - MOVING THROUGH EMOTION

Emotional energy on its own is neutral. What we feel and our reaction to an emotion puts a stamp on it as either positive or negative. Feeling is the subtitle we give it as joy, fear, anger or sadness. When we attach a definition or a thought about the emotional energy, then it takes on meaning.

Our emotional energy is expressed through physical and mental sensations, like pain, fatigue, pressure, etc. These are signs of emotion trying to move on its own to create energy in motion.

Being open to learning how to move through our full range of emotional energy will bring abundant healthy healing.

What healthy healing mechanisms can we use to move through our emotions?

Uncovering and embracing our divine feminine energy creates an opening to allow nurturing and healing. And this energy invites emotion to be fluid, to move in and out with ease, to be receptive to self and others.

Cultivating your awareness to balance both energies is key to a healthy relationship with not only yourself, but with others as well. Some ways to tap into your feminine healing, and to move the emotion, could come from these selected actions.

Make this fun! Tap into Amazon to find an oracle card deck that resonates with you. Setting an intention and pulling a card each day grounds me with clarity on how to define my emotion and in what way to feel it.

Insight Timer, a phone app, has timed and guided meditations to focus on particular emotion clearing. Self-help reading books, podcasts, support groups, therapy, and journaling provide a link into emotional processing.

Physically, finding a yoga practice and/or exercise regime that floats your boat, will certainly move emotion out of your body and into the universe. Healthy food choices with adequate water consumption should positively impact your emotional health. Sticking to a balanced diet, skipping out on all the bad stuff, will promote a happier well-being. What we eat and how much we eat really plays a number on our mood which in turn affects our emotions.

Are you an artist? You don't have to be. Other therapeutic ways to process our feelings to move the emotions through:

- Create a drawing of what you are feeling, use colors, shapes, symbols etc.
- Make a gratitude list - what are you thankful for in your life right now?
- Physically lose control. Scream, cry, rip up some paper in teeny weeny pieces.
- Vent with intention. You got a closet or small enclosed space you can scream in for a few?
- Know when to express yourself, aim for regulation, not repression!
- Keep a mood journal.
- Practice deep breathing.
- Don't hash and rehash a situation that evokes emotion, either in your head or out your mouth.
- Accept reason - when bad feelings overwhelm you, think of ways to make yourself feel better. Reading something funny, walking outside, visiting with a friend or loved one.
- Accept self-forgiveness, practice empathy, be a good listener, cut out distractions, and stay optimistic.

When we absorb negative and unbalanced energy to feed our

emotions, our wheels internally slow down, get stuck, and potentially could be growing into disease or a chronic illness.

In this frenzy, we are unwell, unhealthy, at war with our mutations, ignoring trauma, hold a sense of unworthiness, experience daily fatigue, pain, and unexplained sorrow.

Going down the woo-woo path here. We have seven chakras carefully placed from the base of our spine to the crown of our head. Each one, represented with a color, corresponds with specific nerve bundles and bodily organs.

If one or more chakras are blocked or unbalanced, this shift can impact our health on all levels. Our mission is to keep all these beautiful energy wheels spinning to realize a balanced healthy place of well-being.

Crown chakra: purple
Throat chakra: blue
Heart chakra: green
Solar plexus chakra: yellow
Sacral chakra: orange
Root chakra: red

Personally, and on an emotional level of understanding, I want to dive deeper into two of the seven chakras that have been blocked, and in looking back at past experiences, eventually introduced medical interventions and undesired disease.

Our sacral chakra is responsible for emotional connections, gratification, pleasure, and creative energy, and is tied to how we process our emotions as well as those of others. In looking back at my past actions and wounded emotions, I had a disruption of healthy flow. I feel this neglected energy resulted in me having my daughters via C-sections, and both hips replaced.

Our heart chakra, another emotional center connection, also rules the lungs, upper spine, shoulders and the breasts. Dr. Northup shares:

> "Breasts are the most fundamental form and representation of maternal love and nourishment. But the love that makes maternal nurturance so life-affirming must be replenished regularly—otherwise it leads to health problems in the organs of the Fourth Chakra, often the breasts."

Without awareness of my emotional feeding and processing, each experience or incident had me feeling all the negative feels; resentment, anger, frustration, jealousy, fatigue, lack of physical touch, sadness... My emotional bondage and sometimes outbursts of frustration would secretly feed my breast cancer as an uninvited guest.

This disease opened up my chakras. I am paying attention. I have actively been working on opening up these two energies creating a healthy flow and healing. As one affects them all, I am present in discovering balance in all chakras to stay balanced and energetically healthy.

This healing process did not happen in isolation. I had help from coaches, therapists, and other group support. Some personal notations for me that I want to share with you are: I am learning to tap into my divine feminine, to let go of my masculine ego. I am learning to BE present and not sweat the small stuff. Shit will get done when it gets done. Go with my flow of creativity. In addition to balancing my emotions to reap emotional health, I am developing a stronger intuition, and am aware of shifts in my relationships with people, places and things.

I have opened my heart to forgive, and accept that I am worthy of love and care from others. I am reassured through loving affirmations, mantras, and card pulls that I am on the right path to heal my heart and stay cancer free.

DESSERTS - ALCHEMIZING EMOTION

Emotions bring substance, color and definition to life. Our emotions, when fed a balanced diet, then put into motion with natural healing mechanisms, can transform our life into a healing, breathing experience. Our existence is filled with meaning and value when we experience all the emotions.

Seeking out positive relationships or connections with like-minded people who share an intention of understanding are the ones we need in our corner to positively feed our emotions on all levels. Discovering strong mentors who walk your emotional path can help redirect your walk towards healthy emotional awareness to heal.

A year ago, I found my coach and my sisterhood. A free challenge of self-discovery flowed into a life-changing revelation for me. I was introduced to my divine feminine side which has been hidden for so many years. I kicked my masculine control ego to the curb so I can have fun, be more creative without self-restrictions, awaken my intuition, and just be present without all the hustle.

And most importantly, be open to an emotional rebirth! A rebirth of my healthy healing authentic self. Diving into my human design charting, I discovered my place and role in this reality, which brought an overflowing sense of calm and clarity as to what I am supposed to be doing and why I am doing it.

Through finding my sisterhood and sharing, I realized that I wasn't alone or losing my mind for the way I was feeling or acting. This bond allows transparent space in relationships to be seen and heard, and not cower into isolation. This is real shit, and we are all in it on some emotional level, trying to figure it out with the help and guidance of another or others.

Once we process our emotions to emulate positive feelings, what do we do with them? We are developing a relationship with our emotions in order to flow forward into a place of healing. Finding our personal practices of moving through our emotions should bring a comfortable companionship that is easy to fall back on and trust when you fall into that familiar place of uneasiness. Finding your stillness to turn the negative or painful emotions into beauty, abundance to heal.

Practice makes almost perfect. The more we own our truth and understanding surrounding our emotions, the more grace and gifts we will receive.

On the other hand, now that you have moved it, what do you do with it? How to turn it into an empowering thing? By owning it, naming it, challenging it, and changing it.

I GET TO OWN IT

Emotional empowerment - step up sister! All the years I harbored and packed my emotions tight, I blamed someone else, some situation, some environment whatever. These past experiences did set the stage for my emotional production, but now I have realized that these are my emotions, not someone else's. I need to be the badass of my emotions. I created them and I get to choose how to use them.

I GET TO NAME IT

Calling out emotion and shouting a name puts me in control and takes the power away from the emotion. This labeling brings clarity to what the emotion is, and where it is coming from. If it has a name, then I can file it away for processing, and make a mental note on how to approach it next time.

I GET TO CHALLENGE IT

As I come into power with my emotions, I find I am able to make choices about how I feel. If I am holding onto more than one emotion at a time, I can still challenge and make changes. Take a look at the emotional reaction. Does it seem right? If it doesn't seem right, can you guess where this emotional reaction is coming from and why it is coming up right now? I have the choice to see if there are other emotions, I think would be more empowering or make the situation different. I may or may not find something else. By challenging the emotion, I give myself the opportunity to change it.

I GET TO CHANGE IT

Emotions are choices, and I can change my mind. I can change how I want to feel about a circumstance and then take the necessary steps toward changing it. Some emotional changes will happen instantaneously in a lightbulb moment. Other emotional changes are more deep and complex, necessitating time as well as work to sort out. Whether it takes a long time or a short time, I am able to recognize that the power to change my emotions belongs to ME.

Our emotional connection to all places of well-being; physical, mental, spiritual, and intellectually, is the connection to all things. It is all about choice.

Taking control with personal choice creates an astute awareness of what and how we are nourishing or feeding our emotions; what healthy actions we are taking to move through our newly balanced emotional "meal"; to feel comfortably full with a sense of empowerment. This process of alchemizing our emotions promotes a place of transformation to heal.

Wherever you are in your journey--struggling, surviving, safe, or supporting--keep your emotional compass pointing towards your north star of abundant, healthy healing.[1]

About the Author

Crystal Grenier is an online wellness consultant who helps women thrive despite a chronic illness so that they can realize an abundant life through guided offers around emotional health focusing on six phases of support; building community, e-books, workshops, a membership program, virtual and live retreats, and mastermind courses.

https://linktr.ee/crystalg03

---

1. **SOURCES:**
   https://youtu.be/FlDYsRbUTsE
   https://www.authenticityassociates.com/the-real-purpose-of-emotion/https://www.cypresslakeslodge.com/emotional-empowerment-in-4-steps/
   https://www.drnorthrup.com/energetic-breast-and-heart-disease-prevention/
   https://www.healthline.com/health/mind-body/sacral-chakra#takeaway

IT'S A GIRL!

EMPOWERING FUTURE GENERATIONS BY BUILDING LIFELONG CONNECTIONS

BY BETHANY BAGBY

> "If you want to change the world, go home and love your family."
>
> — MOTHER TERESA

"It's a girl!"

The three words that would change my life forever.

Most moms would say something like that, and all for different reasons.

As for me, I was terrified.

A daughter. What if she turned out just like me? With no self-esteem, no sense of her inherent worth, and such poor body image that she ended up with an eating disorder? What if she spent her life hiding in the shadow of shame, guilt, and fear not believing that her voice matters? I believed that she would be born worthy of all the best this world has to offer, but I couldn't accept it as true for myself.

22 months later, I had a second girl and realized that it was no accident. My biggest fear as a new parent was that I would be too weak to guide my children and would ultimately break their spirit,

stifling their creativity by forcing them into the only mold I knew. The same mold I had been trying to break out of my entire life.

Then, it clicked. Who better to guide these two fierce, independent, and spirited girls?

I grew up in a small town and an even smaller religious, gender role-centric community. When I was around four years old, my grandpa gave me a little red broom and told me that I couldn't come out to the garage anymore; I had to go inside and learn women's work with my grandma. I still remember standing there on the sidewalk by his truck. It was dark outside. Their house on my left and the garage across the open driveway to the right now felt miles away. My grandpa was an amazing man, and he was giving me a loving, heart-centered gift in line with his values. My immediate perception, though, was that I was less-than, and limited, because I was a girl.

I also felt isolated because all of my siblings and close cousins were boys. I realized they would be working and spending time with him, but I couldn't. I would go on to learn many valuable lessons from my grandpa, but we would never have the close relationship he shared with my male family members.

There are many more examples throughout my childhood that reinforced my belief that I was less-than, different-from, and separate. There is one memory, however, that shows the true effect of those beliefs. When I was in eighth grade, we had a career day in our home economics class where a sweet lady asked me what I wanted to be when I grew up. I answered with, cosmetologist, one of the approved vocations in my mind, but I was secretly thinking, "I wish that I were a boy. Boys have choices. Boys can be anything they want to be." This memory has become what some would call a mission moment for me. I never want another child to grow up believing that they are limited because of who they are.

I spent 32 years trying to reconcile who I was born to be against who I thought I was allowed to be and all it resulted in was self-hatred. I do not want that for my children or for anyone else's, and I am committed to helping parents change the narrative.

I felt lost and invisible in my teenage years, not understanding where I belonged or what I was supposed to be working towards. My low self-esteem was only compounded by the fact that I had been obese for as long as I could remember, and was painfully shy. After a sports injury and subsequent surgery, the surgeon told me I had to lose weight because my ankle simply could not support me. While honest, those were crushing words for my fragile psyche to hear. I started doing every fad diet under the sun, running, lifting weights, and continued playing sports. Not knowing anything about properly fueling my body, I was starving myself, but the weight was coming off, and I was ecstatic. After losing 40 lbs, the weight didn't fall off as quickly, and I began taking more extreme and desperate measures.

I would eventually become bulimic, a dark secret that I would hide for well over a decade. I lost 75 lbs. in total, but it would never be enough. *I* would never be enough. But I was good at a couple of sports, so I focused all of my attention on that. If I could never be feminine and beautiful with the body of all those girls in magazines, then I could be physically strong, competitive, and intimidating. That was the mask I hid behind: the defiant, "I'll show them," lone wolf persona that seemingly served me well from an outside perspective. Inside, however, a void was growing.

After high school, I joined the military, which probably seems like a crazy turn of events for a girl who wasn't even allowed to wear pants, but a couple things had happened in those years that paved the way for that course. First, my mom had made an absolute dream come true for me. She is the definition of a woman who can manifest anything and the mother who will do anything for her children. She moved mountains for me to take a 21-day student ambassador trip through Europe. I got to experience this big world that I had no idea existed, and it opened my mind to new possibilities. Thank you, Mom!

Secondly, my two older brothers had joined the military after 9/11 so, in a way, I was following in their footsteps. Truthfully, though,I was running. I had no idea what I was doing with my life, and patriotism seemed like a convenient four year delay in figuring it out. I still didn't understand that I had the power to blaze my own trail.

The military was my first taste of equality, equal opportunity, and diversity. It was a culture shock to say the least, but I still felt the need to prove that women had a place in the military and the world, that we had earned, and deserved, our seat at the table. The words of Clare Booth Luce were my driving force, "Because I am a woman I must make unusual efforts to succeed. If I fail, no one will say, 'she doesn't have what it takes,' they will say, 'women don't have what it takes'." My efforts seemingly paid off, as I quickly rose through the ranks. But moving into leadership roles left me with an extreme feeling of imposter syndrome. Who did I think I was, holding this level of responsibility? Who was I to be leading men and women older than me or with more time in the service than me? Who was I to be leading anyone at all?

Despite my internal struggle, I was blessed with several amazing leaders and mentors throughout my military service. They saw a person with potential, heart, and grit. They believed in me and pushed me out of my comfort zone and into the arena. They empowered me to use my voice at a time when I didn't believe I had anything worth saying. They introduced me to the concept of collaboration over competition and I began to realize that not only could I not do it all alone, I wasn't supposed to. Through their guidance, I would eventually realize that the only person I was trying to prove my worth to was myself, but that watershed moment was still to come.

Over the course of a year, I was screened for a military special program which included all manner of mental and physical testing, including a psychological assessment. When I was cut from the program, one week from selection, I had to meet with the same psychologist for an exit exam. This was the first time I had gone after something in the military and "failed." The psychologist looked over my file and said, "What's next for you? Please tell me you're going to get out of the military and do something better with your life." I was shocked, and he saw me get upset as my mind left the room. He said, "Where did you just go?" I told him I would be 30 at the end of my enlistment and it was too late to start over. To his credit, he didn't laugh at me. Like a wise grandfather, he explained to me that I had the "wattage" to do whatever I wanted and, not only that, but the military is only 1% of the US population, meaning that there are over 330 million people out there making a life for themselves and I could do it too.

This was my watershed moment, the moment I truly believed that I could make my own way. The moment that the possibilities seemed endless.

It's a girl!

The three words that would change my life forever. If the exit exam with the psychologist was a watershed moment, and having my first girl was life-changing, then having my second girl was like someone shaking me to wake up. There was no more waiting, no more wondering, I had to make a change *now*.

By this time, I had met and married an amazing man. When we first started spending time together, it was the kind of encounter where *you just know*. Not love at first sight, but a peaceful realization that your soul has met its match, like, "Oh, I've been looking for you, and you're finally here." We were brought together when we needed each other the most. We became partners in everything, and that accountability in regards to health and nutrition is what helped me finally kick bulimia to the curb. Over the first few years together, we'd face health issues, loss of a grandparent, loss of a parent, and no shortage of other intense personal and professional stressors, but we had each other, and we were elated to learn we were having a baby.

Beyond my initial fears, we were both worried about our careers. Was the military really the environment we wanted to raise our children in? Thousands of couples do it, and God bless them, but did we want to leave our child for deployment-length spans of time? Did we want to be single parents during each other's deployments? I had been in very stressful roles over the years. The kind where you get to work an hour early just to have some peace to read through emails, work feverishly and somewhat frantically all day, only to head home late evening and not be able to turn your brain off and be present with your family. What sleep I was getting was riddled with stress dreams, and I felt in a constant state of fight-or-flight:

jittery with angst and beat down; exhausted mentally, physically, and spiritually.

Now, I have to say that I worked with some phenomenal people in the military who became family. We formed those bonds intentionally. After all, the high operational tempo meant that we spent more time together than with our families. We probably even knew each other better than our families knew us at times. That's great for a positive work environment, but again, was that what I wanted for my family? For my co-workers to know me better than my own children? For a heaven-sent daycare worker to know my child better than me? No, absolutely not. It only added to our collective desire to break away and design our own lives. Every night, there we were, talking about how we hated that our daughter was in daycare all day and that our only time together was the mundane evening routine of dinner, bath, and bedtime.

This wasn't the life we envisioned for our family. So we lay there and wondered: Is it possible, do you think, for a modern family to be so deeply connected that each member of the family feels wholly seen, heard, and valued? I think it's a question with a resounding YES, but we're constantly growing and figuring out how to actually do it. I also think the "how" is different for each and every one of us, because there's no one-size-fits-all way to live your life.

We made the difficult choice and took a leap of faith. We dared to believe that our life could be different. We both separated from the military, sold our house, packed up in a rented RV, and moved our two daughters and two dogs to the other side of the country. I spent the next several months deep-diving into who I am without all the titles I held in the military and all the limitations I felt throughout childhood. I worked with an amazing coach who helped me dissect all my stories, and ultimately realized that I was still trying to live in a paradigm in which I didn't belong. I had to give myself permission to move on. It was painful to let go and grieve the loss of the person I once was, but integral in choosing the woman I get to be, the wife and mother I get to be.

Uncovering my purpose unearthed the vision of a heart-centered business that not only aligns with my values, but empowers families to build lifelong connection, despite the rigors of everyday life. My life is now overflowing with the kind of mindful connectedness I could only dream of before. I whole-heartedly believe that every family can be a ripple that creates change. It all starts at home. It won't happen overnight, but when we shift our mindset to use small moments as opportunities to connect, we can make a huge impact on our families' lives.

This is what I want for every family. That's why I started the Family Unity Project: to give other families access to the tools that transformed mine.

Imagine a life where your family doesn't have to work at connection because it's already woven into the fabric of your lives. Here are two simple practices that can help set that transformation in motion.

THE FAMILY VALUES EXERCISE

One of the first conversations I recommend diving into is discussing the intrinsic values that define what it means to be a member of your family. Not in a limiting way, but in a way that gives your family something to anchor to.

Decide together how you want to be known as a family: as generous, accepting, loving, hard-working, trustworthy, reliable, etc. Everyone gets a say in this. You can even create a mantra or contract that everyone signs and then posts on the wall. "We are the (last name)s. We are ____, ____, and ____."

Consider doing this exercise at the beginning of each year to set the focus for how you want to show up as a family in the coming year.

The reason I love the core values activity is because it sets the foundation for what is truly at the heart of my mission: creating a deep connection that allows each member of the family to feel seen, heard, and valued. When we practice acceptance and learn to honor and celebrate diversity in our own homes, we are giving our children the love, understanding, and support they need to explore who they are as an individual.

DEDICATED QUALITY TIME

Not all discussions or activities need to, or should be, as deep as defining your values as a family. Meaningful quality time only requires freeing yourselves from distraction and enjoying time together. It can be playing a board game, card game, sport, indoors, outdoors, a craft, a conversation, cooking, literally anything that gets you talking and having fun together.

Quality time doesn't have to take hours. In fact, keeping it to just 30 minutes a day can make it easier to shut out distractions and stay actively engaged with one another. The important thing is just to show up for it consistently and stay dedicated to the intention of creating deep and meaningful connection as a family.

When we show up for each other in this way, it changes us. It allows us to see the strength in diversity and the value that each and every person holds, in our family and outside of it. It allows us to step back and realize that we all have different perceptions of the same event, problem, and best way forward. Our individual reasons matter, and they deserve to be considered. This is the ripple that will radiate beyond our homes and into our communities, creating space for us to connect with others on a deeper level.

How different our lives would be, had we grown up learning to communicate and offer understanding to each other as a general way of being. How different would we be if we commit to learning and teaching it now? What a gift to give future generations, and what a legacy to leave behind.

About the Author

Bethany Bagby is wife, mom, disabled veteran, author, coffee enthusiast, and the founder of The Family Unity Project, where she is empowering families to build lifelong connections by creating consistent and intentional time together where each member of the family feels seen, heard, and valued. She is helping parents create unique experiences for their families and finally harness that highly sought-after quality time amidst their everyday, busy lives.Bethany lives in Central Florida with her husband, two daughters, and two dogs. For more ways to connect with your family and join a global community of parents supporting each other on this crazy, beautiful ride we call parenthood visit www.thefamilyunityproject.com

https://linktr.ee/bethanybagby

STAND IN YOUR POWER

BY DR. IZDIHAR JAMIL, PH.D.

> "Stand in your truths and you'll allow others the permission to be the best version of themselves."

> — DR. IZDIHAR JAMIL, PH.D.

I was picking up my son Abrar from preschool, just like any normal day. I was running a little late because I had to feed my baby, Nadrah, who's about twelve months old.

I arrived at his preschool and went straight to his classroom. Of course, Abrar wasn't happy being the last one out, but I explained that I needed to take care of his baby sister before coming to pick him up.

He took his bags, and I pushed Nadrah in her stroller, heading out. Because we were late, the main door was closed, so I went through the dining hall to get to our car. It was lunchtime for the upper grades, so there were a lot of students eating and chatting.

As I was heading towards the exit door, I heard someone shout from behind me:

 "Hey, Suicide Bomber!"

Shocked, I froze. *"Did I hear that correctly? Did someone just call me and my kids 'Suicide Bomber'?"*

I turned around, and all I could see was these hundreds of eyeballs just looking at me in silence. Nobody said a word. I could feel my chest tightening. I couldn't breathe.

"Did that just happen, or did I imagine it?"

But in my heart, I knew it happened. I could see that my two kids just stood there in silence too. None of us knew how to react.

So I gently ushered my kids towards the exit door. We walked straight to my car in the parking lot. As soon as I got into the car, I called my husband and told him about the incident. He was shocked and surprised that an elementary student had the audacity to label us so harshly.

I could feel my heart being broken and shattered. I immediately texted Abrar's teacher about the incident. She was surprised and said she was sorry it happened. She also said that she informed the principal regarding the incident.

The Anger

I got home feeling so angry, scared and heartbroken. All we did was pass through! Couldn't they see that we're just like them: a mom picking up her children, just like millions of other moms do every single day? The only difference was that this mom just happened to be wearing a hijab.

So what should I do? Pull my kids out of school? Report it to the police? Reach out to the media?

I could feel this anger welling up within me, and playing the blame game consumed me to the point that all I could think about was how unfair society is. I became anxious, afraid, and angry to the point that it was affecting my health.

The Turning Point

I made a decision. I'd had enough of the anger and the blame game.

I would not give my power away and let them win. I decided to let things go, knowing that I'd done my best in the situation.

So now I go about my normal routine. I send my son to the same school. Not only that, I actually put more of myself out there by helping out in the classrooms, at school events and on field trips. It's my way of saying, "Hey, this is the true me. Can you see me as I really am?"

I'm someone who loves her community. I'm passionate about children having the best possible education. I'm also a mother who loves her children, and a devoted wife. I choose to take my power back by focusing on what really matters to me: my family and my community.

FORGIVENESS

One of the hardest things I've had to do in order to gain my power back is to forgive those people. I believe that I'm right, which makes them wrong. But being right has a cost to me. Then I realized that it's not about who's right and who's wrong. There's this saying: "You can either be right, or be happy, but you can't be both."

I know what's important to me, and that's being happy. So I said my prayers, I talked things out with the people I trust, and did a lot of breaking and grounding work to free myself from this anger.

Forgiveness isn't for them; it's for me, so I can be free. I keep saying over and over again "I forgive them. I forgive them. I forgive them," until one day it clicks, and I'm free!

THE UNEXPECTED

One day, as I was walking through the car park to pick up my son from school, suddenly, out of nowhere, the school principal jumps out and says, "Mrs. Jamil, I'm the principal here at this school. I just wanted to say that I'm really sorry for what happened to you. I just wanted you to know that the issue has been dealt with!"

I was shocked, thinking, *"Really? How did that happen?"*

When I asked the principal what happened, the principal said that the boy's friend, who heard him saying that to me, said, "That's not okay what you're saying to that lady and those children." He told his teacher, who brought it to the principal for further investigation.

That's when I learned that the truth always comes out. And no matter how bad things or situations are, there is always goodness in people, and that goodness will help you fight for the truth.

The courage of the truth first starts with you. If I had not found the courage to report the incident to the teacher, chances are that it would have happened again.

And I honor the courage of that boy, who found the bravery to say "that's not okay!" I don't know who his parents are, but I have so much respect for, and gratitude to them, for raising such a brave person, one who dares to fight for justice even when it's hard.

Since that incident, for the years that my children have been in that school, that incident has not repeated itself.

Key Lessons

Here are some lessons that I've learned in standing in your power to create a better life for yourself.

#1 - The Choice

Whenever you've experienced a traumatic experience or tragedy, even though it's soul-crushing, know that you always have a choice in how you deal with it. In my case, I choose not to be a victim, and to bring the power back to me.

#2 - The Courage

Sometimes finding courage in a difficult situation can be tough. At times it'll feel easier just to give up. But there are costs for being silent. Find the courage within you to speak up, like when I told my son's teacher what had happened and let her know it was not okay.

. . .

#3 - LETTING GO

Once you feel that you've done your best in the situation, let it go. Allow God, the Divine, to take care of things for you. Focus on your responsibility to yourself, your family and your community. It's easy to hold on to the anger and play the victim, but it'll have a huge impact on the quality of your life and your health. I chose to forgive those people so that I could be free.

#4 - JUSTICE

Trust that somehow, somewhere, the truth will come out. Justice always prevails. Keep on having the courage to be the real you. Trust in the goodness in people, like when that boy told his teacher that his friend calling us "Suicide Bomber" was not okay.

#5 - BEING

Who you are being is the key to creating the outcome you desire. If you're being a victim, angry and blameful, the world that you are going to create will be one of hatred.

But when you choose to let things go, being forgiving, loving and free, the world that you create is going to become that. Your inner world creates your outer world. So choose who you want to be, and that will be your world.

More importantly, plant a seed of goodness and positivity, so that others can live in a world that operates in trust and justice. Just like that boy's parents taught him to do the right thing, even when it's scary. As a result, his actions created a safer, more accepting world for my children and I.

POWER SUMMARY

Let's summarize the key points in this chapter.

1. Fill in the blank. Stand in your _____.
2. Why is forgiveness important?
3. You can be right or you can be happy, but you can't be both.

KEY ACTIONS

Here are some key actions or mini-coaching to help you to stand in your power in a moment of darkness:

1. List one person you are going to forgive
2. Who do you choose to be today?
3. Do one brave thing today

About the Author

Dr. Izdihar Jamil, Ph.D. is an immigrant, Asian, hijab-wearing Muslim computer scientist turned media expert.

She is the 10 x #1 International Bestselling Author of *It Is Done*, *Yes I Can!* and *Women Who Lead.*

Izdihar has spoken at many prestigious events and interviews all around the world.

She was featured on Forbes, TED, Fox TV, NBC, CBS, ABC, CW, Thrive Global and hundreds of media and publications.

In 2021, Izdihar was inducted into the prestigious Marquis Who's Who biography in recognizing her contribution as the top 5% in the industry alongside Warren Buffet and Oprah.

Her TED talk on overcoming social adversity and the courage to be proud of your roots and heritage has inspired many people from various cultures to take a positive step in accepting other people's principles and values.

She is an influential trailblazer and an inspirational leader in helping female leaders to share their voices on prestigious platforms without prejudice.

She has helped over 100 female leaders to solidify their positions as the #1 go-to expert in their fields with her simple, no-fuss methods.

Izdihar lives in California with her husband and three kids and in her spare time she loves reading and baking for her family.

https://linktr.ee/izdiharjamil

SELFISH IS THE NEW SEXY

BY SARAH QUINN

I *want it all, every last drop of temptation explored. Every last drop of desire filled, and every discovery of passion ignited.*

I wrote this in my journal two years ago, and like dominos perfectly aligned, one tipped and knocked them all over in perfect formation.

I wanted it all, and NOTHING was going to stop me.

You wouldn't believe the things people say about you behind your back when you choose to live an extraordinary life.

There has to be a space and time where people learn that the stuff they say never actually stays behind your back. So let me tell you now: It surfaces, Luv. Be prepared for that.

So how does a cold-hearted bitch climb to the top and claim everything she ever desired?

Let me tell you...

I chose to be selfish. Like, right down to the core selfish.

Spoiler alert, it's OK to claim this as who you wanna be. After all, you make the rules for your life. They apply to you and you only, and you get to create whatever you want for your life. No exceptions.

So I choose selfish.

I'll admit, it was hard at first because I felt genuinely bad for saying

"No." Of course that was until I realized that there had rarely been anything genuine about the times I had said "Yes."

I'd done things because they were:

- Age-appropriate
- Situation appropriate
- The way my mama did them
- The way my friends said I should

I'd done things:

- For him (Oh gosh, all the times I had said yes for the "him" in my world, or to get the attention of the "him" I wanted in my world *facepalm*)
- For her
- For them

All of the while showing up feeling:

- Guilty
- Stressed
- Bored
- Tired, oh so tired some days
- Overwhelmed
- Irritated
- Disappointed

And all the while telling myself:

- Next time I'll just say no.
- Why do they always ask me to do this shit, can't they figure it out for themselves?
- Do they even realize what I gave up to be here? Had to do to get here? How crazy the rest of my day/week is gonna be?

Secretly wanting to resent them but ultimately at the end of the day realizing it was all on me.

After all, I was the one who said yes in the first place.

I swear it's like I forgot along the way I had a choice!

Now don't get me wrong: I'm a good friend, daughter, mother, citizen, boss, leader... but ONLY because I want it.

I do what I want, when I want, how I want. The result? I end up helping more people than I ever could have imagined, loving more fiercely, creating depth in my relationships, reaching unlimited wealth and crushing my professional goals.

Most importantly, I've found my secret to unshakable happiness.

Being selfish never felt so damn sexy to me.

To those of you who are rolling your eyes with the many excuses as to why you can't have this too: LIAR. An excuse is an excuse.

Sit with that for a moment.

It's a reason why you believe you can't, shouldn't, couldn't and ultimately don't.

But an excuse is also a belief.

Maybe you need to change things up, let people down a little, do things a different way, but we are talking about YOUR happiness here.

What is that worth to you?

Isn't it worth it to the people around you? I mean, don't they want you to have unshakable happiness?

If the answer to that is no, then Girl, get outta those relationships.

If that person would rather you sacrifice your:

- Peace
- Passion
- Freedom
- Sanity
- Sleep
- Love
- Connection
- Good vibes

- Perfect relationship
- Moments with your kids
- Living your dreams

Just so they can have theirs…

It's time to give them the boot.

You have no obligation to be second to anyone's happiness.

So here we go: selfish is the new sexy.

Ready to claim unshakable happiness?

Here's what you'll need to prepare for,

"Sheesh, I just thought since we were friends you'd…"

This will sting. Of course it will. Because a "good" friend bends over backwards to do whatever her gal pals need from her, right?

Wrong AF! A good friend understands that by helping her when you're already overloaded (or whatever is going on in your world), you are making your own life a living hell, and that's not what either of you wants. A real friend gets that it's not that you don't want to help her, it's that it's just not feasible sometimes, and she loves you anyway. You still cheer each other on and you show up when you BOTH feel good about it!

"Do you think you're better than me/us?"

Perhaps! That's my answer.

If someone asks this, it's NEVER about you. This is THEIR level of self-esteem coming through. People on the personal development train rarely grow to their desired potential because of this right here. They start to grow apart from their friends and family, and suddenly they are the black sheep being shunned and locked outta the stable in the middle of winter. Girl, grab your boots and build a cabin in the woods. Making yourself small for anyone is just plain WRONG!

If someone is implying that you think you're better than them, take it as a sign that you are successfully growing and mic drop that shit. No need to justify someone else's lack of growth or diminish yours. Just thank the trash for taking itself out and move on.

"So what, you're just gonna… (Travel? Leave? Dump him? Quit your job? etc.)"

YES! The answer is a resounding "Yes I am!" You don't need to explain yourself or justify anything. Sure, there are times when you'll want to have logistical conversations when your choices directly impact another's quality of life, but ultimately you owe no one.

You wanna leave your relationship... go!

You hate your job... quit, ask for that raise, change it, couch surf if it makes ya happy!

You wanna travel the world and not have a home base... get your booty on the plane and go! The world won't stop because of this. You'll be ok. You'll figure it all out. If it's what you want, you'll pull it off and keep it together.

And my all-time favourite...

"Don't you think you're being selfish?"

"Yes. Yes I am, and I'm super friggin' happy. Don't you want me to be happy?" Gosh I love this response. I mean, who in their right mind is going to say, "No, I don't want you to be happy"?

Of course, they are going to say yes, unless you've got some bloody rotten assholes in your life, in which case, march your ass out the door and c'est la vie!

It's your party, Girl, cry if you want to, or feel damn good about it. The choice is yours.

If you've ever prayed, "God just give me a sign, I just need to know I'm on the right track..." Um, he's been giving you that sign every day for your entire life. All-day every day. He gave you YOU. Your heart, your mind, your body, your soul. You just keep shutting them up and ignoring them!

Why, Girl?

The secret to happiness is knowing YOU and acting on THAT. Like, *the real you!*

Those passing thoughts about what you should do? Do 'em!

I've experienced extensive trauma in my life. This is coming from a girl who left her kids (oxygen mask on first), lived in a shelter and, trigger warning, experienced various forms of sexual abuse.

So I don't say these things lightly or neglect where you may be at or what you may be faced with. I say them with heart and soul.

No matter who you are, what you've done, what you've been taught, or what you've experienced, you DESERVE happiness.

Today and every day.

Say no when it feels like a no.

Say yes when yes feels good.

Uncomfortable? What can you do to get comfortable?

Scared? What do you need to feel safe?

Lonely? Create some friendships that leave you feeling fulfilled and wanted.

Overwhelmed? Let shit go!

Tired? Take a nap, the world will live if you stop for a moment no matter how much you wanna believe it won't.

The more times you put yourself first, the easier it will get.

Being selfish has allowed me to launch a business that serves thousands of entrepreneurs around the world in a way that I feel incredible about.

What will you do with your selfish?

About the Author

Sarah Quinn is an entrepreneur and writer based in Quebec City. When she isn't furiously unleashing her true message via Facebook Lives, or her podcast, A Poor Coach's Guide to a Rich Life, she is running her online coaching business as an entertainer, speaker and success mentor to coaches around the globe.

With a new series of books, over a decade in online business, and several hundred product and event launches under her belt, Sarah is known as a 'Content Queen' who just doesn't stop. She believes that you CAN have it all, on your terms, so long as you're willing to get honest with yourself about what you're really here to do in the world, and her mission in life is to help coaches learn to use their voice and day to day life as a powerful tool to inspire themselves and others to lead with authenticity, creating a life wilder than their wildest dreams.

Sarah is also a mom of 2 and is obsessed with teaching her children that you can have it all, exactly as you want and on your terms.

Sarah is also an expert in "No B.S" coaching and would love to help you create a business you love, completely on your terms!

https://linktr.ee/sarahquinncoaching

THANK YOU!

Thank you so much for engaging with these stories. If you experienced any benefit, please consider doing any of the following:

- **Leave a Review** on Amazon or Goodreads. Your reviews help prospective readers decide if this is right for them & it is the greatest kindness you can offer the authors.
- Recommend it to a friend.
- Join the Red Thread movement and share your own story in a collaborative author book, or a solo project: www.redthreadbooks.com

Live free, live fully, live feisty!

CALL FOR SUBMISSIONS

Red Thread Publishing is calling for submissions to our *First-time Female Author Anthology: Brave New Voices*.

Write a chapter or a short story, send it to our submission committee, and if selected we will publish it in our anthology & offer our writer's coaching & publishing services to you. **To learn more & send submissions, please visit:** https://bit.ly/3mImp59

If you don't qualify for this project & still want to write & be published, check out **Red Thread's Collaborative Author projects**: https://bit.ly/3v0xQJx

Well we are an on-purpose, for-profit company. It costs money to produce a great book, but we acknowledge that not every voice is bankrolled. We believe every story matters, not just the stories of the women who can afford to publish them. Therefore we have built into our business structure scholarship funds using profits to support organizations for good in the world as well as our first-time authors anthology publishing.

Website: http://redthreadbooks.com/

ABOUT THE PUBLISHER

Stories Change Lives

We believe in the power of women's voices & stories to change the world. We support women not only to write & publish their books but to own their voice, accelerate empowerment & reach global impact. Because women matter.

Do you have a story that must be told?

Sierra Melcher, author & founder of @RedThreadPublishing, & our team will support you every step of the way.

Redthreadbooks.com & info@redthreadbooks.com

Made in United States
North Haven, CT
02 March 2022

16676410R00114